JACKIE VERNON-THOMPSON

TRANSFORMATIVE ETIQUETTE
A GUIDE TO LOVE AND REFINING SELF

Paperback ISBN: 978-1-63616-074-0
Hardcover ISBN: 978-1-63616-078-8
Ebook ISBN: 978-1-63616-075-7

Published By Opportune Independent Publishing Co.
www. opportunepublishing.com
Best-Selling Author Coach: Nikkie Pryce

Printed in the United States of America
For permission requests, email the author with the subject line as "Attention: Permissions Coordinator" to the email address below:

Info@fromtheinsideoutsoe.com

DEDICATION

Everyone has that special someone or a special set of people that have contributed to the person they have become, and I am no different.

Without hesitation, I dedicate this book to my late beloved mother, Aneita McIntosh-Williams. Without my mother, this book would not exist. Without her, I would not be in the position I am now as a confident, God-fearing, and loving woman.

My mother never failed my siblings or me. She made enormous sacrifices to ensure her five children were fed, clothed, and lived in a comfortable and decent home. I am grateful for her love and sacrifice. I am most grateful that from a child, she taught me who loves me more than she could ever, and that is my Lord! She was the full package and the epitome of a loving, caring, and phenomenal mother.

When I decided to begin the journey as an Etiquette Consultant, my mother was the first, without hesitation, to financially invest in my business. She always believed in me and trusted I would follow through.

I owe it all to my MAMA. I dedicate this book to her.

CONTENTS

ACKNOWLEDGMENTS

First and foremost, I am grateful to God, without whom I would not be here. I would not have the opportunity to write this book, let alone become a Certified Etiquette Consultant, and change lives globally, primarily children, on a daily basis. I thank God for loving me unconditionally and giving me the life-changing words to share with you in this book.

I am so very grateful to my husband, Jerome, for his constant encouragement and support through this process. I recall countless conversations we have had in reference to the details within this book and why he believes certain excerpts should be included. Babe, your ideas, and recommendations were such a great contribution to completing this book, and I thank you so very much. I love you, babe!

When I shared with my sisters Karen and Juliett, on a conference call, that I decided to finally write a book, they immediately increased their tone and expressed such excitement. They did nothing but encourage me, as usual. They are my big sisters, and I will forever be grateful to them for their love and support. I love you both so much.

Later in this book, you will learn about my big brother Jimmy who contributed tremendously to me being the person I am today and the strength that I now embody. He gave me a priceless gift that changed my entire life, one he didn't even know he possessed. I can't let the cat out of the bag. You just have to continue reading in order to find out what it is. Jimmy, I love you so much and will forever be grateful to you.

My oldest brother Dalton has always been a cheerleader for me. I chuckle a bit each time I call him. He greets me, almost always, like this, "Mrs. Thompson, How are you?" Even though he is my oldest brother, he has always expressed so much respect for me, and it is definitely mutual. He has encouraged me throughout my life, and he loves me dearly. I am so very thankful to God for my siblings. You can probably guess that I am the baby of the family, not spoiled, just the baby. LOL I love you big bro.

My father, Albert, and loving stepmother, NaVerne have supported and encouraged me through this process. Their love has proven to be unconditional, and I am so very blessed. I remember years ago, having a thorough conversation with my dad in reference to writing this book, and without hesitation, he blessed me and encouraged me to write the best book possible because he is so proud of me. He was not concerned that there might be uncomfortable excerpts in reference to our relationship. He simply desired for me to succeed. I love you both more than you know.

Auntie Millicent literally picked up the baton after my loving mother passed, February 2018. There has never been a week she hasn't called and checked on me. There is never a time she doesn't see me and gives me a huge bear hug. She encourages me in everything I do. She doesn't comment on social media. Nonetheless, she will see a post I've made related to my business or something social and calls, "Jackie, I see that you are doing this or that...I am proud of you!"

Auntie Millie, thank you for always affirming me. I cherish and will love you always, not only because you stepped in for my siblings and me after mama passed, but because you are such a loving and giving individual. You always reply by saying, "I love you more," when I say I love you. This time, I love you more more…! LOL

My Auntie Veronica also immediately jumped into position when my mom passed, keeping the tradition of family lunch after church on Sabbath and so much more. She is always encouraging and never hesitate to express her love for me. When I shared with her that I was writing a book, she immediately expressed happiness for me. I love you dearly.

Dr. Dee Thompson is an entrepreneur who I rub shoulders and interact with often during various networking events. I have always admired her. However, I did not take the opportunity to share my admiration with her the many times we interacted. When I decided to write a book, I was perplexed about a few things and contacted Dr. Thompson to express my endeavor and perhaps receive advice. I found that it was only God Who led me to her because our conversation helped to place me on the right path. Thank you, Dr. Thompson.

My nephew, Chaun and goddaughter, Chante, who without hesitation agreed to become models in the making of my series of etiquette DVDs. It would not be possible without the two of you. Thank you so much for your sacrifice. I love you both. Thank you, Bree, for your sacrifice as well.

I absolutely love my family. Thank you all for your support.

I am eternally grateful to the Clergymen that have encouraged and supported me over the years: Pastor M.M. Young (deceased), Dr. T.A. McNealy, and Dr. Fred Batten, Jr.

Thank you so much my Mt. Olivet S.D.A. Church family for your love and support from childhood to now.

A special thanks to Denise Batten for assisting with final editing.

A special thanks to the Vice Mayor of Lauderhill, Fl - Denise D. Grant. She has given me undying support from the moment she learned of what I do and my passion. She has presented countless opportunities for me to work with the youth by teaching them skills to help transform their lives. She clearly believes in and supports the work I do. I thank you Vice Mayor Grant. You certainly are for the people, especially the youth. You have become a sister to me. I love and appreciate you.

A special thanks to the Mayor of Lauderhill, Fl - Ken Thurston for your continued support and passion to provide the youth resources and tools to excel. Thank you for giving me the opportunity to educate the youth and adults of your city in etiquette & protocols.

I am so very grateful to former Lauderhill Commissioner, Howard Berger for believing in me from the very beginning and supporting us every step of the way.

A special thanks to Chief Constance Stanley and the City of Lauderhill Police Department for their consistent support.

I am grateful to the City of Lauderhill for opening its doors to me and trusting me with its youth. I grew up in Lauderhill and I am blessed to have the opportunity, time and time again to pay it forward. It is so very fulfilling.

A special thank you to the City of Lauderdale Lakes, Fl - Mayor Hazelle Rogers for her constant support as I walk in my purpose. Mayor Rogers, you are so very appreciated.

I would be remiss if I did not express my gratitude to Mrs. Velma Lawrence and the Embrace Girls Foundation of Miami, Fl for believing in and supporting me from the inception of my etiquette school. We have partnered year after year in ensuring the girls of her organization in Dade County elementary schools learn proper etiquette and are positioned for greatness. She and her team are top notch. Mrs. Lawrence, you rock! Thank you so very much.

A very special thanks to my Best-Selling Author Coach, Nikkie Pryce. She has helped transform my life by walking me through this process. She has been such an asset, and I am grateful for her talent and expertise, as well as her nurturing spirit. Thank you for praying for me before each coaching session.
You are the real deal!

INTRODUCTION

The journey to refinement and confidence is seldom easy. It requires, first and foremost, the changing of one's mind from the old way of thinking and executing to a new and completely unfamiliar way. It is an uncomfortable place to exist when you know there is a better way to do things and a better way to conduct yourself, yet, you just don't know what to do or how to do it. There is always that moment in everyone's life when they wish to improve themselves and be positioned in a place where success and progress are inevitable.

It is that moment when you are driven to seek the information, tools, and know how to begin the journey of improvement.

As you read this book, you will see that regardless of what you have experienced, nothing or no one should be given permission to stunt your progress or opportunity to access the resources that will assist you in becoming that person who people enjoy having in their company. No one should stop you from being that person who walks in a room and there is this aura about you that intrigues those in the room or even the person who feels completely confident when dining, interacting, conversing, working or socializing with others.

There is a sense of confidence about you that attracts folks to you who clearly have similar values as you do. They value proper deportment. They value confidence. They value the very essence of one who understands that proper etiquette & protocols are not just for the individual. Proper etiquette & Protocol is also for the folks around them, and it is administered simply to keep order, set safe boundaries, and ensure everyone in the environment feels respected and appreciated.

Regardless of who you are or where you are from, you deserve the finer things in life. You deserve to be viewed as one of quality. And you deserve to be valued.
This fascinating read will position you.
It's time for you to believe it for you.
It's time for you to embrace it for you.
It's time for you to love yourself unconditionally regardless of what life tosses your way.

**REFINEMENT * CONFIDENCE * SELF-LOVE *
SELF CONFIDENCE** are on the way.

Enjoy the read!

CHAPTER 1
WHERE IT ALL BEGAN

Considering how passionate I am about etiquette and all that comes with it, one would ask, "What is it that drives her?" I am often asked the question, "What led you to decide to become an Etiquette Consultant, now an expert?"

The simple answer is, it wasn't my idea, nor was it my decision. It was God's decision and clearly my purpose. I had no choice but to obey.

Allow me to expound on that brief answer. In order to do that, I must share a series of events that took place from childhood to well into my adulthood. This is my perspective and my truth.

At the age of three, my dad left my mom, four siblings, and me and moved to the United States. At that time, we lived in Montego Bay, Jamaica. Our mom and dad had five children, and I am the youngest. At the age of three, all I knew was that my daddy was gone. It was personal for me.

Fast forward to the age of seven, when we moved to Florida. I can remember seeing my dad a few times when he and or his wife, our stepmother Nae, would visit us from Chicago and take us to the circus. I recall once swimming in the pool at the hotel where they lodged. I also recall visiting Chicago a couple of summers and two winters. However, after a few times, that sort of visiting ceased for some reason.

Even though those visits ceased, life still went on, and my mother had to take care of us as she consistently worked two, sometimes three jobs to keep a roof over our heads, food on the table, and clothes on our back.

My father would send financial support for us. However, it just didn't seem to be enough, apparently, because I would wonder why my mom had to work so hard. The more I saw my mom work, the more I became angry at my father. My mom would work two jobs cleaning houses and taking care of her employer's children while taking the bus back and forth, rain or shine, until she was able to purchase a really dated vehicle from one of her employers.

Once she purchased that car, that allowed her to secure another job. Wow! So, this is how the process would go several nights a week. My mom would finish her two jobs, come home and cook dinner. Then we would all jump into the car and head to certain banks and medical offices to clean them as supplementary income for our household. Even though dad sent money to assist, in every other way, she was alone in all of this. She was a single mother doing it by herself. Naturally, I blamed my father for not being there for us, which caused my mom to feel the need to work so very hard.

Over time, my anger for my father grew even more. Mind you, I was angry at him and loved him at the same time. I was extremely angry that my mom had to endure so much burden for their children. "After all, she did not make us by herself," is what I would say to myself. I was angry.

As I began high school, my anger grew to the point where I was literally becoming bitter at the world and people in general. I did not know I was broken. I could not truly identify what was going on. One of the main reasons I could not identify what was happening is that when I would express to my family that I had no regard for my father and that I did not respect him because he left us, they would resist even to relate to or understand my point. I would hear, "Jackie, you gotta get over it" or "You're wrong about him." However, no one ever took the time to sit me down and verbalize what it is that I've got so terribly wrong.

It was no secret. My family knew how I felt about my father. My family knew I was angry. However, no one really took the opportunity to delve into my reasoning and feelings. I don't really blame them because in the Caribbean, more specifically, the Jamaican culture, the mindset is to move on and get over it. It's a cultural thing.

I was sort of in my own little prison dealing with my feelings of detestation and love for the first man God placed on this earth to love and take care of me. Yet, it was just a theory to me and my siblings. My motto for my dad was, "He's a dead beat," which was consistently coming from a place of anger.

After graduating high school, I shared with my mom that I wanted to try to build a relationship with my dad. I wanted to heal that bitterness inside. She agreed with me that it was necessary. I applied to a college in Georgia, which is where my dad and family moved. Shortly after graduation, I moved to their home. My stepmother was always such a sweet and welcoming person. I grew to love her as we spent more time together. She became the best stepmother a girl could have. However, my relationship with my father was estranged and felt very awkward. It seemed to me he knew how I felt about him and had no idea what to do.

There was an elephant in the room that no one would challenge or discuss. The straw that broke the camel's back was when he and I had a confrontation. I cannot remember what the topic or reason was. However, we were shouting at each other, and he asked me, "What do you want from me?" I replied, "I feel you owe me!" At that point, his immediate response was, "I don't owe you a thing!" And it was not said so nicely. Those words pierced my ears and heart. To be honest, I cannot remember what transpired following that statement. Clearly, there was nothing else to be said once he declared that he owed me nothing.

Shortly after that, I decided to return to my mom, the one parent I felt I could rely on and was consistent. I attended college in Florida instead of Georgia and earned a couple of degrees with the love and support of my mom and family.

Even though I felt accomplished, I was still very angry, even more so than before. I became angry at the world. I became bitter, self-conscious, and defeated. All this while, no one really knew the extent of what was going on in my head and heart. I believed the myth that society told me, at that time in my life, that I was ugly because I was of a darker hue. I not only felt abandoned by my father, I also felt abandoned by society because I was not "pretty enough, my skin was not light enough."

These beliefs and feelings led me down a path of insecurity and low self-esteem. My father and society have turned their back on me, is what I thought. One would see me now and disbelieve the latter statement. However, it is all so very true.

I then began to feel that I wasn't good enough to speak up or good enough to remain in a quality relationship with a guy. I would rehearse this crazy thought that "He's going to leave me just like my dad." This literally was a rehearsed statement I made to myself. Therefore, if I were in a relationship with a guy, as soon as I noticed any signs of him acting up or headed to break up with me, I would break up with him first, as if to say, you won't do me like my dad. My family members would ask, "How do you get over these guys so fast?" I would tell them, it's easy, he just wasn't for me, or something to that effect. I didn't care, and I wasn't about to allow him to hurt me like my dad does. It became so bad that I literally had a fear that my brothers would one day become so angry at me for any given reason and abandon me. It was deep y'all, it was deep.

I purchased my first home at the age of 26. At some point, my father heard because someone shared the information with him. However, he never called to congratulate me nor even acknowledged it. I was disappointed and just beyond hurt. I was just shattered yet showing a smile.

I wrote a five-page letter to my dad, not complaining and not blaming. I simply pleaded to him that I needed him as a father. I was yearning for a father-daughter relationship. I wished to have a dad who would probe my boyfriend or potential significant other, celebrate accomplishments, and just have a dad and not just a father. For two months, he did not respond with a phone call or a written reply to my letter. At that time, reluctantly, I called him to ask why he hadn't responded to my letter. He responded by saying, "I didn't know what to say." Again, I was very disappointed and helpless. I realized at that point that I would just continue to be a statistic and bitter.

Fast forward a few years later when I began to sell real estate in addition to my career as a Graphic Designer. I had grown so tired of the bitterness, anger within, and the disdain I had for my father. I grew tired of crying every time someone would ask me if I spoke with him. I grew tired of being heartbroken because I expected him to call or do something I requested. I was literally, at this point, filled with total distain for him. But I still loved him. I don't understand how that could have been. I detested him because he wasn't there for me. He wasn't there for the children he helped bring into this world. He wasn't there for the extraordinary lady who birthed those five children for him. Yet, I yearned for his love and a relationship with him.

THE BREAKTHROUGH

One afternoon I was sitting in my office just doing my usual real estate work, and he came across my mind. I began to think how angry I was at him and life. I began to cry profusely. I needed my dad because I was emotionally and mentally a wreck and just broken due to his absence.

I could not control the tears flowing. A voice said to me, "You've got to get control of yourself because someone will notice you." At that point, I decided to call my big brother, Jimmy, just to talk. Even though I expressed my great disappointment in my dad over the years to my family, I could still speak with Jimmy about anything. So, I called my brother while crying. He alarmingly asked, "What's wrong?" I simply said, "I am tired of being angry with dad. I'm tired." Immediately my brother apologized to me for consistently disregarding my pain and concerns about the absence of dad. He said, "Let me tell you who dad was before he left." He began to tell me the fun and special things dad would do with us and for us. During Christmas time, he would take us downtown to see the Christmas lights. He would buy us ice cream and so much more. He said dad was there for us before he left. I could not believe it. Because he left when I was three, I had no recollection of what my brother mentioned. I hadn't recalled a single moment with him.

For the first time in my life, someone really heard my cry. For the first time, someone, my brother, Jimmy, took the time to tell me that my father loved us so much that he ensured my siblings and I had a good time over and over and he was there for us up until he moved away. He even said, "Dad loves you, Jackie."

Immediately following my brother's statements and sharing with me that our father loved and loves us, it seemed as if a huge burden fell off my shoulders. A still small voice said, "See, your father did love you at some point, at least."

For the first time in my entire life, someone took the time to assure me that my father loved me. Wow! My father actually loved me. That was the realization and revelation that took place that day. Just knowing that information, was lifechanging for me.

FORGIVENESS

Immediately, right there in my office, the detestation and anger turned to pure love and forgiveness. I cannot explain it. I had no idea that all I needed my entire life was someone to share with me something my father did to demonstrate that he loved me at some point. I WAS SET FREE THAT VERY MOMENT!

There was one more step to take amid my freedom from the anger and unforgiveness. I had to humble myself and reach out to my father to tell him I forgave him. There had been tension between us for many years. We have been estranged, and I just didn't trust him because of his consistent absence.

That very night, I arrived home and knelt at the side of my bed. I prayed for strength and courage and cried. Then, I picked up the phone and dialed his house number. To be honest with you, I did not expect him to answer because usually, my stepmom would answer when I called. I would speak with my dad perhaps every 6-8 months because we just didn't have much to say to each other.

In any event, he answered this time. I did not greet him. I did not ask him how he was doing. He said hello. I simply said, "Dad, I forgive you." His response was, "I've been waiting for this call for years." For the first time in my life, I truly felt as though my dad wanted me. I was astonished that he had been waiting for me and I was that important to him. This was quite a bit for me emotionally.

I asked him why he wasn't there for us…, for me? He shared with me that his father wasn't there for him, and he didn't know how to be the father we deserved, and so much more.

Keep in mind when I called my dad and shared with him that I forgave him, I didn't say that with the expectation that he would change. I was not expecting a different person because I know regardless of what I do, I cannot change anyone. I can only change myself. Not only that, but I decided that I was going to begin to love him without hesitation. I forgave him with the intention of accepting him for the father he is, not the father I believed he should be. I did not expect to have the greatest relationship with my dad suddenly. That was unrealistic. I went into forgiveness mode and called him with absolutely no expectations or intent except to simply inform him that I forgive him because it already took place in my heart. Listen, apparently, all I needed was to know that my father loved me at some point in my life. That was good enough for me. That little piece of knowledge that my brother shared with me gave me the power to release anger and disappointment and begin to love my father.

I chose to allow us to begin developing a very pure and organic father-daughter relationship as a result of that phone call. I made the effort, and he made the effort as well. He lived in Georgia at that time and I in Florida. However, we regularly spoke via the phone.

I was like a kid in the candy store. I finally, in my adulthood, had my dad. I began to love him without anxiety and could not imagine my life without him. I just totally opened my heart to him, for him to fill that gap that existed far too long.

Eventually, my dad and stepmom moved to Florida within a 5-mile radius of his 5 adult children. For the first time since I was 3 years old, we live in the same state and, better yet, in such close proximity.

It was such a wonderful thing. This move has allowed me to draw closer to my dad, which allows us to develop an even higher quality relationship.

When I call my dad or vice versa, my heart leaps when I hear him say, "Hello, my love," or "Hello, my beautiful daughter," in his Jamaican accent. The love is pure and authentic, and I feel it.

I love my dad because without him and my mother, I would not exist. I love him because, despite the bitterness and anger toward him that I housed in my heart for so many years, and he knew it, he loves me anyway. He just didn't know how to demonstrate that love effectively. I accept that.

DIDN'T WANT TO LET IT GO

Honestly, I don't know if my dad had attempted to draw close to me before I forgave him, would have made any difference. I married the anger, bitterness, and detestation. Even though it was painful and emotionally exhausting, I was comfortable there. It was weird. I was functioning in my dysfunction, and it became my excuse for being angry at the world and mean to folks that didn't even deserve it.

The time finally came for me to release it, and God made it so very easy. He said it was time.

Now, I know everyone's story will not end like this, where you develop a beautiful relationship after forgiving your father or mother. Why? Because everyone is different, and some may not be emotionally or mentally ready for such a change. Everyone's story is different.

WHERE'S MY HUSBAND?

I would be remiss if I did not share this significant part of my story. Before I forgave my father, I was open to meeting that man God had for me. Ladies, I was ready to get married even amid my anger and bitterness toward my father. I was willing to push that part of my life aside to make room for my husband. I was ready.

Can you believe that? I actually thought I could compartmentalize anger, bitterness, and disappointment and produce true and pure love for a husband. I was fooling myself. I thought I could do it.

I don't remember what I was doing at the moment. However, I heard clear as day, God say, "Until you begin to truly love the first man I placed in your life, I will not provide the man I have for you."

I was again blown away. I heard God loudly and clearly. Sadly, at that time, forgiveness was not yet a reality for me because I did not have what I didn't know I needed until my brother, Jimmy gave it to me.

I did not share the words of that whisper with anyone. I kept it like a rare diamond that I could not touch. Forgiveness of my dad did not come for years after that whisper.

It wasn't long after my transformation through forgiveness, God revealed my husband to me. We dated for six years. We broke up four times, partly because I still had work to do. I came from a broken place and now attempting to develop a quality and genuine relationship with this man who literally showed up at my church door, truly took some work. God delivered him and I met my match. LOL

Eventually, we reunited and now have been married for almost 10 years, pressing forward in true and unapologetic love with the love and grace of God.

I was free to love…

IT'S ON YOU NOW

I know for sure that you must, for your freedom and happiness, forgive your father or mother for abandoning you. Forgive them because it is the right thing to do. Let go of the expectations you have placed on them. Be rid of that voice that tells you they should do this or that. That is what is breaking your heart. BEGIN TO ACCEPT HIM OR HER FOR WHO THEY ARE AND NOT WHO YOU BELIEVE THEY SHOULD BE. Love freely with no conditions or expectations. This is literally a matter of life or death.

If you do not apply what I have recommended, every decision you make as an adult will be dictated by that sense of insecurity you have due to the lack of love from your parent. You will begin to enter relationships with insecurities if you haven't already. You will never be good enough for yourself because you still feel that sense of abandonment. You will never be able to completely walk in your purpose with a free and light heart, because of that bitterness and anger are occupying space in your heart and mind.

You may not know where that parent is. Forgive them anyway. Your parent may have passed, and clearly, you cannot reach them, forgive them anyway. Tell God you forgive them.

DEAR MAMA/DADDY

If your parent has passed, or you just don't know where they are or how to contact them, I recommend you begin a Dear Mama or Dear Daddy journal. In this journal, the first writing should be, "I forgive you, mama, mommy, dad, daddy or however you would like to address them.

From there, as often as you like, go to the journal, and write to them all that you wish you could literally tell them. Share with them what happened during the day, about their grandchildren and other family members. Tell them about your accomplishments and anticipated events and activities. Share your feelings because that is your time and space for you and your parent, who you have now genuinely forgiven.

My mom passed on February 16, 2018. That was the most painful time for my family, especially, my siblings and me. I was advised that one way to cope with the loss, was to begin a Dear Mama journal. It has made a significant difference in my grieving process. It has helped me heal and establish that newfound relationship with the memories and love of my mother.

Now I am sharing it with you. Regardless of where your parent is, if you are unable to establish a physical relationship with that parent you forgave, I recommend you begin your journal.

REMEMBER, even if you can contact them, understand that they may not react in a welcoming manner, and that's ok. The goal is to become free of the hurt, forgive your parent, and experience true happiness, just like I did.

"No More Tears, Dad!"

"I love you with all my heart!"

CHAPTER 2
PURSUING MY PURPOSE

Now that I have forgiven my dad and we are working on our relationship with no expectations, I am free to move into my purpose, whatever it may be.

I began to mentor girls who were growing up in single-parent homes, primarily single mother homes. I joined the Big Brothers, Big Sisters program of Broward County and mentored several girls over the years. It was so very empowering that I was able to impact their lives positively and assist them in forgiving and accepting their father for who he is, among other advantageous adjustments.

I will never forget my times with them. I learned that my story was an aide to so many trapped in that hatred or bitterness mode due to the absence of a parent, and it didn't matter their age.

THE PEARLETTES

While mentoring the young ladies of Big Brothers, Big Sisters, I took leadership of a girl's group of the Women's Ministries Department of my church, Mt. Olivet Seventh-day Adventist Church in Ft. Lauderdale, Florida. The group was called Pearlettes.

We met every other Sunday for years. Each year new and returning students were installed, and the program was always a success. It would be year around bonding, nurturing, and attending events.

During our sessions, the girls would learn how to be a lady, speak properly, take care of themselves, maintain their personal hygiene, and so much more. It was fantastic. I held that position for several years because I was positioned to make a difference.

STILL NOT FULFILLED

Somehow though, I was still not fulfilled. Something was missing. I had been a Licensed Real Estate Agent and doing very well income-wise. I was also a freelance Graphic Designer. So, it wasn't that I lacked finances. I was just not fulfilled, and I knew, without a doubt, I was not walking in my purpose.

So, I began to pray and ask God to reveal to me my purpose. I would talk with God regularly about this subject. However, he did not reveal it to me until a particular Wednesday evening. You see, I was on my way to church when I made a final plea to God. I said, "God, I know You have more for me to do. Please reveal it to me."

He did not answer at that moment. I arrived church. I sat in the pew and began to listen to the service. As my Pastor began to speak, the Holy Spirit stated, again as clear as if He were literally sitting beside me, "When you arrive home, sit still so I can speak to you." I nearly jumped. LOL

I was very anxious to arrive home. After service, I did not hang around to chit-chat. I went straight home, took my shower, and laid myself in the bed.

THE REVELATION

Just before my slumber, while my husband was in the living room, the Holy Spirit said to me, "I want you to start an etiquette school and create etiquette DVDs. I was in awe. Remember, I wasn't asleep. It wasn't a dream. It was a revelation!

Mind you, I had never ever uttered the word etiquette. I was not teaching etiquette; at least I didn't think I was. However, in retrospect, I was teaching it to the Pearlettes and my mentees and didn't know.

I rested so very peacefully that night. The next morning, I asked my husband to join me in the living room. I revealed to him what transpired, most importantly, the message God shared with me before I fell asleep last night. His immediate response was, "Well, if God said it, we have no choice but to obey." I was elated he was on board, and my journey began.

It was clear to me that forgiveness of my dad was required in order for me to be where I am now.

LET'S BECOME LEGITIMATE

I had no idea there were etiquette schools out there. Nevertheless, I began extensive research on the subject and found several nationwide, and not only that, I also discovered you could actually become certified. Oh my Goodness!

To make a long story short, I became certified by two etiquette institutions. I learned quite a bit about etiquette. Through prayer, I took every step necessary to establish a viable and thorough business. I secured models to create eight separate DVDs on eight different topics of etiquette. I wrote the scripts and prepared myself mentally and physically for the new journey. I hired a videographer, and together we created an eight DVD series. This was what God said He wanted me to do. That was accomplished, and I was very happy about it.

God revealed the school to me, January 2014. God even gave me the school's name, From the Inside-Out School of Etiquette, with the assistance of a dear family member who suggested a portion of the name. After positioning the different components of my new business including, a marketing plan and curriculum for the classes, it dawned on me that God had been grooming me all along when he positioned me to be a mentor and the Director of Pearlettes.

It is now confirmed that I had to experience what I did with my father, in order for my purpose to be completely revealed to me. Wow!

I AM NOW WALKING IN MY PURPOSE! I am completely fulfilled because every time I change a person's life by teaching them proper conduct and civility, something sparks inside of me. This is why I am here, to serve with a story and a passion for helping to improve people's lives, whether child or adult.

CHAPTER 3
WHAT REALLY IS ETIQUETTE?

We have grown tremendously by the grace of God, and there is no stopping.

Etiquette is a buzz! Following and demonstrating proper protocols is something every refined person does. There is no way a person can consider themselves refined without demonstrating proper etiquette, and guess what? Proper etiquette is needed in everything we do. Unfortunately, many have no regard for etiquette. That is why some feel society is in such disarray.

Let's discuss the meaning of etiquette. Wikipedia states, "Etiquette is the set of conventional rules of personal behavior in polite society, usually in the form of an ethical code that delineates the expected and accepted social behaviors that accord with the conventions and norms observed by a society, a social class, or a social group."

In essence, we follow a set of rules and protocols to avoid offending our fellow human beings. There are etiquette protocols in absolutely every situation.

In a nutshell, that is what etiquette is. It is not a challenging definition. It's quite clear. Even though it is a simple term, it makes a significant difference in society when exhibited. It doesn't matter if you're in a social or professional setting, an informal or formal setting; there are protocols. There are protocols when you are in the company of just one person or a group of people.

I advise my students always to be conscious of their behavior because it will affect their neighbor one way or the other.

Before we leave this section of the book, I advise you to be conscious of the fact that etiquette varies depending on the culture. Every culture calls for different protocols. For example, in the American culture, it is customary to shake hands, whether male or female, once they meet each other. However, in the Judaism culture, a gentleman typically does not shake a lady's hand. This is said to avoid any sort of physical affection that might lead to transgression. Another example is, in the American culture, it is acceptable to shake the leader of the country's hand with no problem. However, in England, it is forbidden to touch the Queen unless she extends her hand and invites contact. Let's go a step further. In America, we teach our youth to look folks in the eyes because it shows confidence and respect to the person of whom they are speaking. However, in various areas of Africa, if a child looks an adult in the eyes, it is viewed as a sign of disrespect. Typically, children are taught never to look an adult in the eyes in the African culture. The interesting thing is that once or if they migrate to America, they must adjust that etiquette protocol to demonstrate effective communication.

So, you see, every protocol is not acceptable in every culture. However, there are etiquette protocols established in every culture. Keep in mind, because other cultures' protocols are different, it certainly doesn't make them weird. They are simply different and must be respected and valued as well.

That is the reason when preparing to travel abroad, you do research to ensure you are aware of the essential protocols to prevent offending someone or embarrassing yourself. If you ever wish to know a particular protocol in a culture, ask Google. LOL

CHAPTER 4
MINDSET

Everything we do or say begins with a thought. We often hear folks say it wasn't even a thought. I don't understand how I did that or why. That's not completely accurate because, before execution, your mind communicates to the mouth, legs, arms, etc., and instructs it to fulfill your desires. At which point, you can decline the temptation or that small voice in your mind telling you to do this or the other.

That is the same experience everyone has when they choose to demonstrate proper etiquette or not. Everything starts in your mind. When you demonstrate proper etiquette, it is simply showing concern for those around you and making every effort to prevent offense or awkward and undesirable circumstances.

Let's consider a scenario. So, you are in a relationship with your boyfriend, and somehow you begin having communication issues. Regardless of what you say to him, the conversation becomes a huge argument. You become so very frustrated with him and ***decide*** the next time he blows up on you, you will do the same. This is your rationale. Clearly, it is not the right thing to do. However, you're sick of it.

Keep in mind all of this is determined in the mind, first. So, the same night you get into an argument about a very minute issue, and he begins to shout at you. At that point, you make a conscious decision to shout in return. You go a step further and call him "stupid" because you feel at that point, he is stupid. You know for a fact he doesn't like being called names, but you just want to cut him deeply with your words.

You made a conscious decision that you would not be civil with him or demonstrate proper etiquette because he sure isn't. All the while, there is still a voice saying, "That wasn't right; it will hurt him more." As a result of that argument, both of you went in separate directions and refused to speak with each other.

The interesting thing is, if you or he decided to be concerned about each other's feelings and show civility, you might not have found yourself in such a predicament.

If you had only decided to demonstrate civility and proper etiquette and responded to him differently, you would have perhaps calmed the situation and had more favorable results. So, you see, taking full responsibility for our choices to obey or disobey our thoughts is paramount. Simply begin to think of others in everything you do and say, bearing in mind that your actions will impact them one way or the other.

That is essentially what etiquette is! So, let's break it down in simple terms. After research, my basic definition of etiquette is, **"Conducting yourself in a manner that doesn't offend those around you"**. Therefore, you would be aware of what you say and how you say it. In the above scenario, if either one of you thought about this word etiquette and the meaning, you would not have called him stupid, and he would not have been shouting because both would demonstrate proper etiquette and civility and show more concern for each other's feelings.

When you desire to demonstrate etiquette, you are always concerned about your attitude and how you relate to people. For example, if you desire to exhibit proper etiquette, you would be sure not to use profanity, especially in public, because it may offend anyone within the hearing of your voice who is uncomfortable with such language. You would not knowingly place people in awkward positions. And because we are not perfect, we are as flawed as they come, which is simply being human, if we happen to offend someone by any chance, we are to acknowledge it, take responsibility, and apologize for the offense. It is not your responsibility to then make the person accept it. It is all now on that person, not you. This, too, is proper etiquette, attempting to make what went wrong, right.

SHIFT YOUR MIND-SET

You now know what etiquette is. It is time to shift your mindset to have the desire and motivation to exhibit proper etiquette. It is one thing to know etiquette protocols, it is another to demonstrate them and make it a lifestyle. You want to be conscious of your behavior and be interested in making attempts to demonstrate proper etiquette in all circumstances.

Let's make this very clear! You are not "bougie", which essentially means you are trying to be upper class or seem better than others. There is nothing "bougie" about exhibiting proper etiquette. It is simply being refined and carrying oneself properly and respectfully.

Do not ever accept the negative connotation that comes with that slang, "bougie". It is meant to break your spirit. Just because you are speaking properly, behaving respectfully with consideration of others, dressing appropriately as not to offend anyone due to exposure, or dining in such an admirable way, doesn't mean you are "bougie" or feel you are better than anyone else.

It simply means you are on the road to refinement, or you are so polished because you believe you are good enough and you deserve to be refined.

Now, bear in mind, there is a thin line between being confident and being conceited. Never use your refined behaviors as a weapon against anyone or to cause someone to feel they are invaluable or not worthy to be in your midst.

Proper etiquette calls for one to humble themselves and to always treat people with respect. You should always be an asset to someone's life and not an entity that breaks them. So, even though you are poised, polished, and refined and have worked so diligently to develop those behaviors, it doesn't make you any better than the next person. That is why humbling yourself is paramount.

As you leave this chapter, you must begin to believe in your heart of hearts that you are good enough to be refined. You are good enough to develop quality and long-lasting relationships. You are good enough for the finer things in life. It only matters if you believe it. So, do yourself the biggest favor and love yourself enough to invest in your improvement and refinement.

CHAPTER 5
SELF-ESTEEM BOOST

As you shift your mindset, you must ensure your esteem is shifted as well. There is no way you will feel as though you deserve to demonstrate all that I am about to share with you if you do not have HIGH SELF-ESTEEM.

Self-esteem is simply how you think and feel about yourself. It has nothing to do with what people think or how they feel about you. It has everything to do with how you feel about yourself. So, let's talk a bit.

First, you must, if you don't already, truly begin to love yourself. This is something I had to learn to do after forgiving my dad. I had to mentally undo all that I had internalized for so many years; believing the lie society told me that I was ugly because of my complexion, feeling as if I was not worthy of being loved by a man, and simply feeling I was not good enough.

I literally had to work on myself to get to the point where I authentically believe I deserve to love myself, and I deserve to be loved. Daily I spoke uplifting words to myself and daily I made the attempt to hold my head up regardless of challenging times. I began to position myself in places where I was subjected to learning something new for advancement. Believing in myself and embracing the fact that I deserve love and success was my focus. Listen to me closely, "You are good enough!" Regardless of what you have done in the past, and I mean the past could be an hour ago, you can change, and you can shift your mindset and begin to love yourself enough to make better choices for your life.

It doesn't matter how terrible it was or how long you have greatly disliked someone, you can change that. Look at how far I came with my dad. That was not an easy thing to do. It took me decades.

So, to have high self-esteem, you must unapologetically love yourself and believe you are a person of value. Listen, do you know you are on this earth for a purpose? God has something that only you, yes, you, can do. Yeah, people can perform acts similar to what you are purposed to do. However, they cannot do it the way you were created to do it.

Can you imagine the enormous amounts of sperm released from your father and only one, just one, attached itself to that one egg your mom ovulated, fertilization took place, and approximately nine months later, you were born? Not only is that a miracle by God, that also says you are here for a reason. So, perk up and get ready to change your life, your mind and your esteem, and position yourself to apply what you're about to learn and have already learned in this book and walk in your purpose.

SYMPTOMS OF HIGH SELF-ESTEEM

- When you have high self-esteem, you are not threatened by the successes of others. You are quick to congratulate them on their achievements.

- You are not easily intimidated by anyone because you know you're good enough to be in the room, sitting at the table and expressing your ideas, thoughts, and agenda. Yes, it is all done with respect and poise. However, you do not hold back when it is time to speak up.

- You do not hesitate to make necessary decisions. Sometimes, you may have to allow the information to marinate for a while. Nevertheless, you will unapologetically make the decisions necessary.

- You will not focus on the mistakes you've made in the past. Listen, no one is perfect. We all make mistakes and will make mistakes in the future. It's human. The important thing is we learn from those mistakes and make every effort not to repeat them. Don't dwell on them because doing that will break your spirit and certainly affect your self-esteem.

- You will understand, embrace, and believe that no one is any better than you and that you are no better than anyone. We are just different people doing different things at different points in our lives. NOTHING, and I mean nothing a person does, makes them any more important than you or anyone else. Bearing that in mind, you can converse, interact, and engage anyone at any level because you believe YOU ARE GOOD ENOUGH!

These incredible symptoms may creep up on you. You may suddenly notice your attitude towards yourself changing, and you're stepping out in life with a smile and energy, welcoming the great things in life.

You may even sit back and hear yourself expressing your ideas in a business meeting. Normally you would be absolutely quiet, timid, and intimidated by your colleagues. However, you sit up and speak up! Yesssss!

CHAPTER 6
HONOR YOUR BODY

I often mention this fact to the ladies I teach, whether young or seasoned, that "Every female is not automatically a lady." A lady demonstrates ladylike behavior and is concerned about her conduct.

Some females decide that they do not wish to demonstrate ladylike behavior, and they wish to do whatever they desire, however they desire and whenever they desire. Ultimately, it is everyone's choice. Once she decides to reject the option to be a lady, she cannot wear the title lady. The term lady cannot be placed on everyone. One's conduct and demonstration of etiquette will inform the public whether you are a lady or not. You don't even have to say a word.

It is the same with our gentlemen. Every male is not a gentleman. Notice the breakdown of the word "Gentle man."

A gentleman knows how to treat the lady in his presence and takes care of her. Just like the lady, a gentleman doesn't have to verbalize that he is a gentleman. His conduct will speak for him.

YOUR APPEARANCE

Understand that your appearance speaks volumes. Every day you dress, keep in mind, you set the tone. Your mirror is your best friend. Take the time to use it by making a 360 in front of your mirror after dressing. Check your front, sides, and back to ensure everything is tucked in and appropriately fit and you are presentable for the public.

Moreover, take the time to do your hair. It doesn't matter if it takes a significant amount of time to style your hair; take that time. If you need to wake earlier, set your clock in order to have sufficient time to do your hair. If you can do it the night before and tie it with a scarf or wear your hair bonnet while you sleep, do that.

Your outer appearance tells the public how to treat you. You set the tone! An associate of mine worded it this way, "People will treat you, the way they perceive you." Point blank.

If I see that you are wearing a hair bonnet and pajama pants in the store or out in public, I am going to conclude that you do not care how you look, and you certainly are not open to opportunities. I am simply accepting the message you chose to send to me, a member of the public, a member of society. Therefore, I will read the message you sent and determine whether I should engage you or go in the opposite direction.

I know what you may be thinking. "She is judging me. That's not fair." You're absolutely correct. It is judging. It's not fair—however, it's reality. If you're honest, you will admit that you judge as well, and generally use a person's exterior to determine your next move. Some may say it's discernment. So, yes, people judge every day. Sometimes it's for the good and sometimes for the bad, like judging whether it will be beneficial to hang with this or that group of friends or whether it's best to head home. We make judgment calls every day. Others may say it's that gut feeling leading them to make the right decisions. Whatever you would like to call it, we rely on it.

That's why you may see that handsome and well-dressed guy standing across the room, and you determine at that point that you must find a way to meet him or interact with him somehow. On the other hand, you may see him, and judging from the way he appears, you determine you're good where you are. See, we make those judgment calls daily. With that in mind, why do you think someone would not judge you when you show up in public as if you did not care. If you don't care, the public won't either, and I guarantee you will miss out on opportunities you could have received had you presented yourself respectfully and decently.

Allow me to bring it home. If you slept in it, you have no business wearing it outside. It should not be worn outdoors if it is meant for in-house, including bedroom slippers and any footwear that resembles bedroom slippers. Yep, I said it. Unfortunately, the fashion industry has sold this narrative that wearing bedroom-like slippers in public is acceptable. That's not true, and sadly so many of our young ladies are deceived by that narrative. When in public, it is not always about comfort. Appearance trumps that. Your clothes communicate. I beg you to take responsibility for the messages you send to the public with your appearance. It can determine your future.

LADYLIKE APPEARANCE

Believe it or not, there was a time when I did not care what people thought of me, and I would wear whatever I wanted. Pretty much, I dared someone to say something to me about my clothes. It was almost like I dressed in whichever attire, knowing it was questionable because I was angry at the world. I wished someone would try to reprimand me because I was going to let them have it. Yes, that used to be me until I learned and began to understand the difference between a lady and just a female and I became free of the bitterness.

As I learned more and more about etiquette and what a lady really is, the adjustments became quite easy for me. I loved the new look and style. I realized being a lady doesn't mean you have to be covered from head to toe. However, a lady is conscious of what she exposes or doesn't expose.

She realizes that her dress or skirt should not be so short that she can't even gracefully stoop to pick something up without exposing herself. She understands that her shorts should not be so short that they leave no room for the imagination. That's not how a lady should dress.

A lady's shorts should be at least 2 inches down from her crotch area to prevent exposure or obvious prints. They should not be so very tight it ends up in every crease. It is imperative she shops for respectful attire that will communicate to the public that she respects herself.

Remember, the stores do not care about you. They care about the bottom line, and that is financial gain. They want to sell as much as possible to have an increase. They are not focused on your future and the opportunities you may or may not have due to your appearance. Therefore, I remind you of the concept called Supply and Demand. When you buy a product, that means you are demanding it. When the industry, store, factory, etc., see that you are demanding it, they will supply more. As long as you or I, the consumer, buy, they will supply it until a change of season or new ownership takes place. Understand, we, the consumers, in many cases, have the power to dictate to the industry what most of the stores should provide with the power of our dollars. That is why you must realize you have buying power.

You can dictate to the stores what is to be on their racks and what shouldn't be there. I have seen stores completely change their look and fashion items because they were not selling as they expected. Just like anything else, they had to shift. Take back control. Shop where there are clothes that speak respect and honor. You make the decision, no one else.

If you find the fashions in a store inconsistent with the message you are trying to portray, shop elsewhere. It's that simple.

ELEGANCE AND CLASS ARE IN!

I don't know of a lady who doesn't want to be elegant and classy. Now, keep in mind being elegant, classy, and ladylike doesn't mean purchasing expensive clothes is required. Absolutely not! It simply means when you wear your clothes, they should properly fit you, be clean, be appropriate, and show that you respect yourself and others.

They should not be revealing and seductive. They should say you took time to prepare your attire, and you considered the message.

Ladies, it's ok to wear your skirt or your dress at knee-length or even below the knee. Listen, I absolutely love to wear my pencil skirts and even dresses with that pencil look. That's simply when your dress or skirt goes below the knees, and as it gets closer to the knees, it becomes smaller as if to hug the knees and fit you more attractively. Give it a try.

When you're wearing your shirts, try to be sure your cleavage is not exposed because it doesn't lend to the ladylike image you are attempting to portray. Ladies, there are so many fabulous shirts out there, and some may be revealing. I recommend you purchase different color camisoles (undershirts) to wear under the shirt to cover your cleavage. Then, you can wear whichever top or dress you like, knowing you will not expose your cleavage, and you can maintain the ladylike image.

I know there are tons of really cute sheer shirts in the stores, and folks can see right through. Ladies, it is inappropriate for a LADY to wear it with just a bra. That is when wearing a cami is most appropriate to cover your UNDERgarment and look ladylike and still feel attractive.

BRA STRAPS BATTLE AND MORE...

Sometimes, you may desire to wear a particular type of shirt like a cross-back shirt, and you just don't have a cross-back bra or strapless bra. That is when you decide to refrain from wearing that shirt until you can purchase an appropriate bra.

Unfortunately, there are countless women in stores and various places wearing her cross-back shirt with a regular strapped bra. The straps of her bra are exposed and just look inappropriate as if she said, "I don't care." Ladies, that's not ok. We should care. If you don't have the right bra for the shirt or shirt for the bra, refrain from wearing it. I say the right shirt for the bra because I have witnessed some of our beautiful ladies wearing cross-back bras with a regular shirt, and in the back, you see the bra crossing at the top just below her neck. You might say I am looking too hard. LOL Frankly, it is obvious.

Keep in mind, a lady must consider her entire appearance from head to toe. I literally mean to the toe. In addition, a lady never leaves her home with chipped nail polish or dirty nails. That is not appropriate and not ladylike.

If your nail polish is chipped and you don't have the time to redo it, simply remove all the remaining polish, be sure to clean and file your nails and go natural. There is absolutely nothing wrong with going natural. This also goes for the toes. Keep them clean.

Everyone doesn't wear nail polish, and it is not required to be a lady. However, keeping your nails clean and filed is required if you consider yourself a lady. Remember, whether you notice or not, someone is observing you. They observe your good, bad, and the not so attractive.

Since we're on the topic of nails, oh my goodness! What is going on? It is not professional to wear extremely long decorative nails. Ladies, society is setting you up when they make you feel it is best to have those extremely long nails with every type of design and color. Those nails will more than likely not make it to the top of the corporate ladder because so much is riding on your appearance. It is not considered ladylike either.

Listen, one of the richest and most revered persons in the world wears her nails completely natural most of the time or very neutral nail polish, and her nails are sometimes as short as the length of her fingers. Can you guess who that is? Ms. Oprah Winfrey.

So, I was watching the Oprah Winfrey Talk Show years ago, as I often did. Something drew my attention to her nails. If anyone watches Oprah, you know she uses her hands, particularly her fingers, to make gestures when speaking. Her fingers grabbed my attention, and I noticed her nails were of a natural color and very short. They were very clean and manicured, of course. I noticed they weren't long and outrageous like society is teaching the girls and women to wear them. Her nails were lightly painted and clean. I immediately said to myself, "Wow! If the richest woman in America wears her nails so plain and only at the length of her fingers, that simply means I don't need to be so extravagant to get to the top, wearing those long nails. Less is better. Less speaks louder than drawing attention to the wrong thing that is so loud (long decorative nails). From that day, my mindset shifted, not only about nails but about life in general. I realized that everything society accepts as the norm is not always the most beneficial for me, who strives to be a lady and who strives for excellence in everything I do.

I know you may wonder if a simple thing like Oprah's nails changed my mindset. It was the significant and profound message it sent. It was deeper than just the nails. I learned a valuable life lesson. Of course, I am always open to learning something that will advance me. For some reason, at that moment that significant message, truly resounded.

So, back to my point, it's ok to wear moderate-length nails. That will help to get you to the top more than those long inappropriate decorative nails. If you wish to excel, your conduct and appearance matter along with other attributes. Be wise with your decisions when selecting your attire and determining your overall appearance. One small thing can distract and deter a person from your qualities. It can cost you an opportunity.

Sometimes we are called to adjust once we learn a better or more appropriate way of doing things. It's ok to change and become more poised, refined, and conscious of your appearance.

Now, class and elegance are not difficult to attain. However, with that status comes discipline, responsibilities, and consistency. They also come in a package. Along with wearing elegant and classy clothes, your conduct must align with the look.

If you behave inappropriately and think you will be considered classy and elegant, you're kidding yourself. Clothes speak; however, your conduct can dispel that message the clothes send, as well.

I encourage you to try your very best to conduct yourself accordingly and watch how you begin to feel about yourself, and for a bonus, you will see how people begin to see and feel about you. The thing is, you don't tell people you're classy, they will recognize it and deem you classy and elegant. It's just one of those things.

GENTLEMEN

Gentleman, the same goes for you. You set the tone as well. There's no better sight than to see a well put together gentleman. Just like a lady must make an effort to maintain herself and be a lady; guys, you should as well. Remember, just because you are a male doesn't automatically make you a gentleman.

Your appearance speaks volumes too. It is not a one-way street. There are protocols for both male and female. So, guys, please don't feel excluded and certainly don't feel etiquette protocols don't pertain to you as well. Everything in this great read, except what is specifically for ladies, applies to you. So, let's chat a bit, gentlemen.

A man demonstrates gentlemanlike behavior to be deemed a gentleman. How you carry yourself will tell the public whether you are a gentleman or not. Your appearance also advises the public on how to treat you.

I must admit, guys have it hard nowadays, especially our black and brown brothers. That means you must make even more of an effort to be that gentleman we are discussing.

You, too, must take pride in your hair. If you wear a short cut, maintain it. If you have twists or dreads, take the time to get those twists freshly done when needed and take the time to get that tapered look around the parameters of your hair to show that you are maintaining. No one is recommending that you cut your dreads or twists. However, it is extremely important to maintain a clean look and a manicured shave if you grow a beard. Essentially, you should maintain yourself because it speaks.

GIVE WHAT YOU DESIRE

Remember, a lady wants a gentleman just as much as a gentleman desires a lady. Both genders (lady and gentleman) desire to have someone on their side who compliments them. So, don't feel you can appear and conduct yourself however you would like and expect folks, potential employers, or your potential significant other, to accept you any way you present yourself. That's not how the world works. You give what you would like to receive.

So, gentlemen, make the extra effort to maintain. If you cannot afford to visit the barber, learn to cut your hair, and taper it or make a deal with a friend that you both learn and cut and maintain each other's hair. Your future literally depends on something seemingly as simple as the maintenance of your hair.

I cannot recall seeing anyone at the top of the corporate ladder or in executive positions looking unkempt, having their hair unkempt, and appearing as if they don't care. One must make a conscious effort to get to the top or in a certain position and status. Those opportunities do not accidentally happen. "You attract them." Let me say that again, "You attract them!"

Guys, pull up your pants and wear your belt at the waist. If I see another guy (young or seasoned) wearing their pants below their buttocks, I am going to SCREAM, an inner scream, of course. LOL That presentation sends the most unfavorable message to the public. It simply says you don't care, and everyone should accept you the way you are. It also sends a message, "I don't think I'm good enough for that opportunity you have for me, so, skip me!"

Essentially, that's what you're saying. Remember, opportunities don't die. They simply move on to the next person who's ready and willing to take them. Your appearance can tell a person whether or not you are ready for the opportunity they have available.

I want to drop a little nugget here. Ladies and gentlemen, I implore you to wear your belt. There was a time when everyone wore a belt if their garment had loops because it was the appropriate thing to do. Then suddenly, so many of our guys stopped wearing belts. Now, out of nowhere, many women are not wearing their belts either. Folks, a belt is a detail, and it is always good to be a detail-oriented person. You could be dressed nicely and elegantly. However, if your garment has loops and you're not wearing a belt, your outfit would seem incomplete, as if something is missing. Clearly, a belt is required. I encourage you to get back into the habit of wearing your belt. It looks better. It speaks!

Ladies, we have many different types of belts. There are many fashion statement belts. Keep in mind; a belt is not necessarily to keep your garment up. That is not always a need. However, the belt, if there are loops, completes your look. It's that simple. It completes your look.

I encourage you to wear your belt, if your garment has loops.

TO CARRY OR NOT TO CARRY MY SHOES

Sometimes we wear our heels to work or an event, and we keep a pair of sandals in our car to change into after everything is over because Lord knows, those pumps, strapped shoes, etc., hurt after a while. That is totally understandable. Sometimes I can't wait to get to my car or get to a place where I can discretely make the switch.

Now, there are a few things I will share with you. I've talked about appearance and conduct quite a bit. This is one aspect of conduct that I need my ladies to really hear.

I highly recommend that you do not place your bare shoes in your pocketbook with everything else. Keep in mind that everything you step on outdoors is on the bottom of your shoes. That includes germs and anything else. Nor should you place your hand at the bottom of your shoes because all those germs, etc., will end up on your hand. You may not see them, but trust me, they're there.

Your shoes, whether sandals or heels, should be carried in a shoe sack, the very least a gift bag or some sort of nice bag, not a plastic bag. Carrying your shoes in a plastic bag doesn't lend to refinement or elegance. Many times, when we purchase our purses, they may come with or in a sack. You can use that as a shoe sack. You can also go online (Amazon, etc.) and purchase a shoe sack. They're out there. You can then place your shoe sack in your large bag until you are ready or leave it in the car. Whatever you do, I don't recommend placing the bare shoes in your bag.

In addition to that, a lady doesn't walk around with her shoes in hand without them being in a shoe sack or a nice little bag. So, once you take those heels off, place them in the bag after removing the sandals or flats from the bag. And please, don't walk barefoot unless you're on the beach, at a pool, or at a place where it is appropriate. Casually walking barefoot outdoors is not ladylike.

Having all this information I mentioned, if you desire to be a lady or gentleman, there should be nothing holding you back because you now know. Let's do it! Position yourself in a place where success, respect for self and others, and demonstration of excellence are inevitable.

CHAPTER 7
SITTING & WALKING GRACEFULLY

I often witness ladies sitting in a way that says I don't care, or I don't know how to sit. Sometimes I am tempted to bring it to their attention. However, I know that correcting a perfect stranger in most environments is certainly not proper etiquette. I believe you should have a relationship with a person to position yourself as one who corrects them or make recommendations. Whether it's teacher and student, personal, or professional, there should be some level of relationship to be comfortable enough to gracefully correct or advise someone to change the way they do things. So, in my own way, I just keep it moving. LOL

Sitting is a big deal for ladies. Notice I am not saying for a female? If one wishes to be a lady, she must realize that one of the most significant indications that a female is a lady is how she sits. Your position when sitting is telling.

Let's discuss it. A lady should never sit with her legs open, whether she's wearing a dress skirt, shorts, or pants. You see, being a lady doesn't only depend on your attire. Being a lady is a lifestyle. Therefore, the objective of a lady, especially when sitting, is to keep her legs closed.

Not only that, but a lady should also not sit crossing knee over knee. No, a lady should not cross her legs because depending on what she is wearing, she can very well expose her undergarment (spanks or underwear) or even expose her outer thigh and everything that comes with it. One may say, suppose I am wearing pants. It's the same protocol. I say practice the correct way, regardless of your attire, so that it will be a natural behavior.

Let's look at this scenario. Monday through Friday, you're wearing slacks to work for comfort and constantly crossing your legs because you're "Not exposing anything". On Saturday and Sunday, you go out, and you're wearing a dress. Because it is so natural for you to cross your legs, you then cross your legs, forgetting you're wearing a dress, and you expose yourself. That is the very reason I recommend you practice not crossing your legs at all to prevent mishaps like I just mentioned. Again, it's a lifestyle.

Finally, a lady doesn't sit and throw one leg over the other leg like guys. That is a sure way of exposing yourself. In addition, it certainly doesn't look ladylike at all. In a nutshell, sitting with legs open is only appropriate for the guys, not the ladies.

I invite you to take a look at the following two photos.

INAPPROPRIATE SITTING

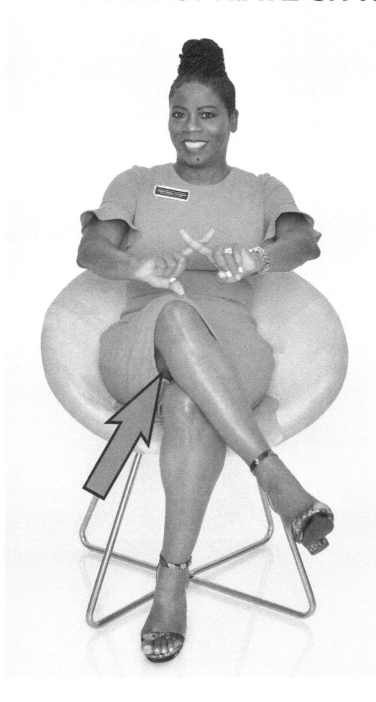

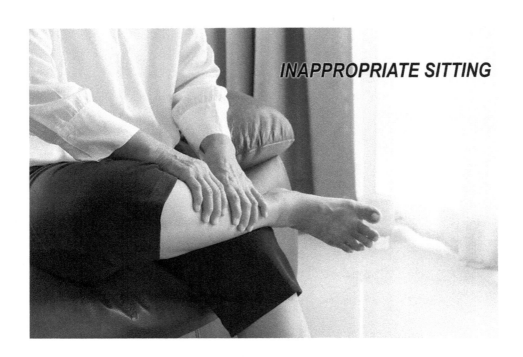

INAPPROPRIATE SITTING

SUGGESTED SITTING POSITIONS

There are a few ways to prevent exposure and certainly sit like a lady, and I will share them with you.

CAMBRIDGE CROSS

The Cambridge Cross is very common when a lady sits locking both knees, sitting at a slight slant, and crossing her ankles. That position is most definitely a lady-like position.

CAMBRIDGE CROSS

DUTCHESS SLANT

The Duchess is another way a lady may sit when she locks her knees and locks her feet, and then she slants both to prevent onlookers from seeing directly up her skirt or dress.

DUTCHESS SLANT

SLANT CROSSING ANKLES

This position is when the lady slants her body significantly, whether right or left, then crosses her ankles. When crossing her ankles, she uses the foreleg to cross and pull the other foot back to align with her buttocks. So, when in that slanted position, her feet must be aligned with her buttocks. All the while, the knees are locked to prevent exposure.

STRAIGHT FORWARD

A lady may also sit straight forward with knees locked and feet locked. When sitting in this position, it is important to be conscious of where you are sitting.

Let's say you are sitting on an elevated stage where someone can look straight ahead at that little peep hole where your skirt or dress stops at your knees. Gracefully slide into the Duchess Slant or Cambridge Cross to prevent that direct view.

I know there is so much for a lady to be aware of. That is why I mentioned at the top of this subject that it is a conscious decision to be a lady. Don't become discouraged. Eventually, it will become a natural behavior. It won't automatically or accidentally happen, though. Discipline and effort must play significant roles in this lifestyle.

I invite you to view this video
https://www.youtube.com/watch?v=9OGXJxNwUWo&t=7s

ENTERING AND EXITING A CAR

When speaking of a lady exposing herself, it is no small subject, whether exposing the top or the bottom. Exposure is exposure, and ladies do not expose themselves. A lady is graceful and poised. She leaves room for the imagination.

A lady finds every way possible to conduct herself in a graceful and ladylike manner, understanding that every behavior is noticed and judged. It's not to say she must be someone else and pretend for people. It is important it becomes her authentic self or it will not last. It cannot be forced either. It certainly can be taught to a willing party. That's what I do daily. I teach young and seasoned women how to be a lady. There is a significant difference, and they realize and feel it from the very first class.

Another way a lady can show herself to be a lady is how she enters and exits a car, SUV, etc. A lady makes every effort to keep her legs closed. That is her objective when sitting anywhere. I don't believe anyone would argue with that.

Therefore, when a lady attempts to enter a car, whether she is the driver or passenger, this is the appropriate way to do so.

She would walk toward the car. Once the door is open, she turns away from the car, with her back toward the seat. She would then sit in the car, hold on to the dashboard and or seat or the steering wheel, if she will be the driver. She would raise both legs together, knees locked, feet locked. Then, swing both legs in together, leaving no room for exposure and having legs tightly closed. That is how a lady enters a vehicle.

Rather, most will walk to the car and open the door. Then, place one leg in, sits, then swings the other leg into the car. That process certainly causes your legs to be wide open and certainly leaves a pretty good chance of exposure. A lady would not wish to expose herself. Even if wearing pants, sitting with your legs open is not ladylike.

So, now that you know, the next time you head to your car, take a moment, and turn away from the car and proceed with the process explained above.

When it is time to exit the car, she would do the very same thing and swing-out both legs together. Both legs should land on the ground together. I advise you to hold on when swinging because you will use your abdominal muscles and need that support. So, hold on, please.

Suppose you are entering a high vehicle or a large truck or SUV; the same protocol applies. However, before you sit and swing, step up one leg at a time as you normally would, hold on, turn and sit, then swing both legs in together. Regardless of the height, whether low or high, you either sit in a low or standard height vehicle or step up and proceed with the protocol.

Now, I know everyone cannot physically enter or exit a car this way because of medical reasons, pain, etc. I recommend you find a way to consciously enter and exit your car leaving very little opportunity for exposure. It certainly is understood if you must enter one leg at a time because of medical reasons. That doesn't say you are not a lady. You are just unable to apply that ladylike protocol. That is totally understandable.

Whichever way you decide to do it to prevent exposure, I recommend you practice it as often as possible so that it becomes natural for you. Trust me. I do it daily without a second thought. It certainly wasn't that way initially.

I invite you to view a couple of our videos on the topic: https://www.youtube.com/watch?v=vgy0leoGiCs&t=79s

https://www.youtube.com/watch?v=widserxs3eQ

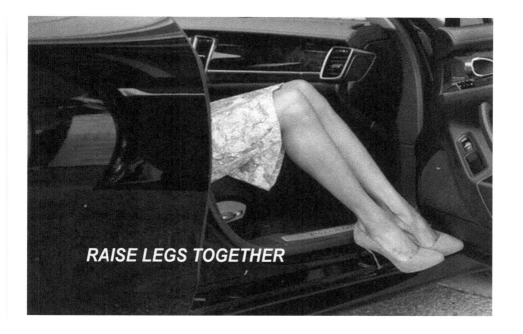

RAISE LEGS TOGETHER

PROPER POSTURE

What exactly is posture? It is simply the position in which you hold your body when standing, lying, or sitting.

I won't belabor this topic because everyone essentially knows that proper posture benefits the body and your entire presentation. Somehow, it is one of the most challenging things for many to exhibit and maintain at any given time.

Trust me, sometimes I catch myself slouching a bit, especially at home, and I must remind myself to sit up and sit properly.

Proper posture can exude confidence, or it can demonstrate that you have no confidence. When you are walking with shoulders dropped in a slouched position, it states you are not confident, and are just moseying on through your day.

Just like everything else, your posture speaks, and again, it helps people to determine if they will engage you or not. Another message improper posture sends is that you do not care about your presentation. That is how it seems. On the other hand, you may indeed care. However, because you may not have been taught the importance of proper posture, you always thought the slouched position was acceptable.

Exhibiting improper posture also inhibits your spinal cord from being in an intended position, which is best to prevent long-term damage and permanent slouched position. You definitely do not wish for your spinal cord to be permanently set in an abnormal position. You may not know this, but your spinal cord has three natural curves-at the neck, mid-back, and lower back. If you practice proper posture, you will help maintain those curves. If you slouch consistently and practice improper posture, you can add curves where they should not be. According to Cleveland Clinic, "Good posture involves training your body to stand, walk, sit and lie to place the least strain on muscles and ligaments while you are moving or performing weight-bearing activities."

There are multiple beneficial reasons one should sit, walk, run, or lie with proper posture.

HOW TO EXHIBIT PROPER POSTURE

One of the most effective ways to ensure you are walking or sitting properly is to roll your shoulders back and drop them. By doing that, your shoulders will be correctly positioned, and the goal is achieved.

When sitting, be sure, as much as possible, to push your buttocks to the back of the chair sitting upright. When you do that, be sure to have even body weight on both hips, or you may feel some discomfort because of the imbalance. In addition, try to keep both feet flat on the floor or in positions I mentioned in the Sitting Gracefully chapter.

I must give you the heads up, though. If it is customary for you to sit in a slouched position, and you finally decide to sit up straight and exhibit proper posture, you most definitely will feel some discomfort because your back muscles are not accustomed to that position. Realize that year after year, you may have been sitting improperly. Therefore, your body conformed to that position. Now, you're telling your body, "I want to train you to sit differently." You will get push back from your body. However, over time, your body will then conform to the new position to help you remain consistent in the proper position. They say, "No pain, no gain."

Another way to ensure you are exhibiting proper posture is to be very mindful, especially at the beginning of your efforts to sit with proper posture. Sometimes you have to say to yourself, "Sit up, sit up." Do whatever you need to do to remind yourself to sit up.

Sometimes, when I am sitting upright in one position for a lengthy time, I begin to feel a level of discomfort in my back. I simply switch positions, still maintaining proper posture. By switching, it shifts the weight and strain from one part of your body to another.

Also, you learned in the Sitting Gracefully section, that you should not cross your legs. Crossing your legs certainly does not distribute the weight evenly. It essentially switches the weight to only one side and more than likely will cause discomfort or back pain. So, relax and consider your positioning!"

When it's all said and done, it is crucial that you practice proper posture for so many reasons. I'm really hoping these tips will help you do just that. It affects everything about your delivery, appearance, and of course, your health. Your posture speaks!

PROPER POSTURE

WALKING GRACEFULLY

As you exhibit proper posture, it is extremely important that your walk demonstrates confidence and poise. I have encountered countless beautiful ladies who are clearly polished and concerned about their conduct. However, they were never informed of the graceful manner in which to walk, or they have never been informed of the importance of walking with confidence, proper posture, and aiming their feet in the right direction.

Unfortunately, many ladies walk with each foot aimed in opposite directions. They will have one foot aimed to the right and one to the left without considering they are not going in the right or left direction. They are headed straight. Regardless of where you walk, whether you turn left or right, you will go straight. Therefore, it is crucial for a lady to walk with her feet pointed directly ahead.

Sometimes you must think and say to yourself, "Feet straight feet straight" to achieve this objective over time.

FEET AIMED FORWARD

WALKING WITH PROPER POSTURE

As you walk, be sure to demonstrate proper posture. You certainly don't want to walk with your posture in a slouched position because, just like everything else, it speaks. When walking in a slouched position, the message that is sent says you are not confident and have zero desire to show enthusiasm or any sort of energy. Now, whether that message is accurate or not, it doesn't matter because it is perceived by the folks you interact with and approach, as not being confident, etc.

Therefore, you must stand erect and walk erect, having your shoulders back aligned with your ears. Again, if you have a challenge positioning your shoulders, simply roll your shoulders back and drop them. That will always assist in properly positioning your shoulders.

You should also be sure to hold your head up where your chin is parallel to the floor, and you are looking straight ahead with confidence when walking. Try not to look down unless you are looking for some cash. LOL Don't be stiff, though. Relax and look ahead toward the prize.

In general, when walking, hold your head up, showing confidence and illustrate to those around you that you are ready for any opportunity that comes your way.

Confidence speaks! I don't know anyone who doesn't value confidence unless the goal is to keep you back or confine you.

With that said, hold up your head, roll back your shoulders, aim those feet forward, maintain a welcoming smile, and shine.

I invite you to view this walking exercise video
https://www.youtube.com/watch?v=mx3uxuzKKdA&t=40s

CHAPTER 8
EXUDING CONFIDENCE

I touched a bit on how your posture exudes confidence or not. As a lady or a gentleman, not only do you want to exhibit proper posture and the other protocols mentioned, you also want to be sure you exude confidence. A confident person attracts confident people.

Now, remember, there is indeed a thin line between being confident and being conceited. So, let's eradicate that word conceited because that has no place in this entire equation. Being conceited means you are vain and think you are better than others. So, nope, that's not what you wish to be.

We wish to be confident not conceited. When a person exudes confidence, they are saying to the public, "I am ready for opportunities available to me!" It also states that you believe you are good enough.

Listen keenly. You need to have confidence. If you don't, you will limit your success or even delay it. Most folks appreciate a confident person. I must tell you, though, there will always be a few folks who are threatened by your confidence or have issues with you because of your confidence. Do not allow that to discourage you or keep you back. In many cases, they wish they were like you. They may not be bold enough to step out like you and exude confidence. In fact, if you find that to be true, take the opportunity to encourage and help them achieve confidence. Sometimes, a person just needs to be validated with words of affirmation. It is also important that people have confidence in you. It makes my heart well when I hear someone say, I have confidence in you. I believe in you. It motivates me to continue being the confident person I have come to be. However, it is crucial, first and foremost, that you, my friend, have confidence within yourself.

As you begin to apply the advice given, you will indeed begin to feel good about yourself and begin to believe and know you deserve to be dressed and presented in a ladylike or gentlemanlike manner, and you deserve to have access to the finer things in life.

Here are a few additional tips to help you become confident:
Avoid negative thoughts and negative people. The words people say can make or break your spirit and, consequently, your confidence, if you allow it.

Not only that, if you feel confident about a project that you are working on, I highly recommend you do not share it with everyone because one negative word from someone can cause you to lose confidence in yourself and your project. It can even cause you to quit. When it all comes to fruition, then feel free to share. That's my recommendation.

I know of people who plan to start a new business. They share the idea with everyone who would listen because they are so excited. They happen to share it with a particular person, and the response is, "I don't think that will work because…" Immediately, they are discouraged and begin to second guess themselves wondering if they can really do this. All because of the naysayer in their ear.

So, preserve your -confidence and press forward, keep your plans to yourself, and inform only folks with the resources to bring it to fruition. This is real talk!

If you're ever going to make a presentation or do something that requires practicing or rehearsing, do it. Don't go into a situation feeling unsure because you have not practiced. That is a recipe for failure or disaster, and that certainly will impact your confidence. So, prepare, prepare, prepare, in order to give yourself a fair chance to shine, and trust me, your confidence will leap.

I believe this piece of advice is the most important of all. Surround yourself with positive and confident people. Those who influence you the most should be at a level or status where you endeavor to be or where you have arrived, and their impact will only enhance you or catapult you to the next level. Also, try to develop a relationship with a mentor, someone more advanced than you and who is genuinely interested in your betterment and progress.

I cannot tell you how crucial it is to have your influencers be people of positivity and confidence. It is motivating and makes you feel as though you can accomplish anything and achieve your goals. I cannot even imagine the opposite. So, reevaluate the closest folks to you who are influencing you the most. It could be family, friends, etc. Sometimes you must somewhat distance yourself from individuals who prove to be detrimental to your development and advancement. You must set boundaries to lessen the impact and influence they may have on you. You must take this task into your own hands. Of course, in the process, demonstrate proper etiquette and be kind. Know you are in control of the decisions you make, and you are in control of who and what you allow to influence you. It's time to step up for you.

Also, to help increase self-confidence, begin to shift your mindset where you believe you can grow, and you can be that positive and confident person you need to be. Believe it and press forward. Be the influencer and encourage people to feel they too are good enough. Become contagious in the most positive way!

FORGIVE YOURSELF

Finally, remember, you are not perfect. In fact, no one is. With that in mind, don't expect perfection from yourself. Be fair to yourself. Forgive yourself for whatever you have done and give yourself a chance to grow and become the person you wish to be or begin the journey to becoming that person, that entrepreneur, that business owner, that wife, that mother, that student, etc.

Give yourself a break and forgive yourself!

CHAPTER 9
PURSE ETIQUETTE

This is a very light topic, however, a significant subject. Understanding how to hold and wear your purse is a pretty big deal, considering that MOST, if not all, women love purses, handbags, and any type of carrier.

I absolutely love purses. I have every type of purse, clutch, long strap, short strap, no strap, chain strap, fabric strap, cross body, handheld purse, etc. I love them all because they accent my outfit daily. Of course, every lady has that everyday purse that holds everything, including the kitchen sink. LOL You know what I am referring to, right?

As we go from event to event, meeting to meeting, we will switch purses to match and compliment what we are wearing. The funny thing is many times I switch purses and take items from my everyday purse and always seem to forget something, like my Driver's License. I know, not good. LOL

Nevertheless, a lady must always carry her purse. A lady never leaves her purse behind, even if you carry just a hairbrush or comb, chap stick, lip stick, debit/credit card or some sort of ID. Ladies, if you are at the age of menstruating, always have a backup pad in your purse because you never know how your body will react to stress and cause your menstrual cycle to begin early. You just never know. A lady is always prepared with a backup pad, and I mean always.

For these very reasons, a lady should wear a purse or handbag.

If you desire to show yourself to be a lady, you must demonstrate ladylike behaviors, from your communications to your everyday conduct and how you simply maneuver this world.

Now that we've got that out of the way let's discuss further, purse etiquette.

When meeting someone, which in the American culture, mainly include handshaking, when safe, wear your purse or handbag on your left shoulder if it has a strap. Or you may hang it on your left forearm. If there is no strap, you may also hold it in your left hand, clutching it firmly in hand.

When you wear your purse on the left side, it leaves the right hand free to shake hands. Remember, your right side engages people when meeting them, so you want to leave your right side free. You certainly don't want to wear your purse on your right side. You may lean in to give a handshake, and your purse swings and hits the person. That's not proper etiquette. Even if you hold your purse in your right hand, you would be forced to switch the purse to the left hand when it's time to shake a hand. That can be quite awkward.

To prevent all the mishaps and awkwardness, I recommend you always wear your purse on the left side or hold it with your left hand.

It is not recommended that you wear your purse directly under your arms, in your armpit. That's not hygienic. Need I say more?

Now, depending on the occasion, you may wish to wear a cross-body purse. You would do just as the name says, rope the strap across your back and front, hence crossbody. This leaves both hands free, and you may shake hands as much as you like with no hindrance and you can do whatever is necessary having no concern about in which hand your purse should be held.

WHERE DO I PLACE MY PURSE?

Some folks find it easy to place their purse or handbag on the floor at any given time. Some may place it on surfaces that are not very clean or surfaces they are not sure are clean. That has certainly happened to me a time or two in the past.

We sometimes don't even think about it. Now, think about coming home from a long day of work. You're exhausted, and you just wish to sit and relax. As soon as you enter your home, you drop your purse on the table with keys and all.

Essentially, what just happened is every type of germs or substance that were on the bottom of your purse or handbag are now on the table. It is the place where you and your family perhaps eat; the place where you may have guests over and dine.

NEVER EVER place your purse on a table regardless of the table. Unless you have purchased that table solely for your purse, make every effort not to place your purse on the table.

Another place I recommend you do not place your purse is on the kitchen counter. The same scenario exists. The kitchen counter is where you prepare breakfast, lunch, and dinner. That's where you chop your vegetables, etc. The germs from the bottom of your purse may truly contaminate what you are preparing. Even if you place a chopping board on the counter to chop your vegetables, etc., it is just too close for comfort. Germs travel.

I recommend you find other places to land your purse or handbag. Somewhere that will not directly affect your system. I go a step further and use sanitizer wipes and clean the bottom of my purse because you just never know. Even then, I still don't place my purse on the counter or table just in case I did not wipe away all the germs. As I said, you just never know.

I also recommend you never place your purse on the floor or any unclean surface. I hope this was an eye-opener for you. I'm not advising you not to place your purse on the floor because you might go broke. LOL I respectfully, do not support that superstition.

Finally, if you have personal items in your purse, e.g., a pad or medication, be sure to zip or close your purse or the pocket where those items are kept. It is improper etiquette to expose these personal items to the public. Plus, I don't think you wish to have folks in your business, right?

Clearly, you see now that it indeed matters where you place your purse. You have been advised on the best side to carry your purse and where you should not place it. When you heed this advice, you will indeed demonstrate proper purse etiquette.

CHAPTER 10
DATING & REQUIRING CHIVALRY (SHIVALRE)

Chivalry is the combination of qualities expected of an ideal knight (gentleman), especially courage, honor, courtesy, justice, and a readiness to help.

He ensures the lady in his presence is comfortable and satisfied before he ensures his comfort and satisfaction. Essentially, the gentleman in your life is to make every effort to treat you in such a way that you feel valued and appreciated.

Now, don't get me wrong. Life is not perfect. There will always be ups and downs in a relationship, and nothing will be perfect. However, the foundation and the general deportment of a gentleman should communicate that one of his top priorities is to demonstrate chivalry, of course, along with other necessary positive behaviors. So, please don't misunderstand and believe all your guy needs to do is demonstrate chivalry, and he's good. There are so many facets to a relationship. Both partners have responsibilities. In this read, however, we will discuss chivalry and what to expect or request from your significant other.

Chivalry is a word that is seldomly used and, dare I say, seldomly practiced. Now that you have gained the confidence you need, or at least you know how to gain that confidence, you may be at that stage in your life where you are interested in establishing a solid relationship that may perhaps evolve into marriage. I want to share a few basic etiquette protocols to look for in that gentleman you are considering. Let's call them dating tips.

DATING TIPS

Because you have or are attempting to apply everything I mentioned in this book thus far, it is crucial, when ready, you seek to develop a relationship with that guy who is refined or on his way to refinement and one who can appreciate you as a refined lady. He should at least have an interest in learning refinement and learning or exhibiting chivalry.

This is imperative because you now know your value. You deserve to be treated like the valuable and worthy lady you are. Therefore, the gentleman on whose arm you will be, must understand the dynamics of that and compliment you just as much as you are to compliment him.

Never become so desperate for a companion that you will lower your **realistic** standards and accept one who doesn't treat you with respect and dignity.

Effective communication must come into play. Knowing now that you deserve this special treatment, before getting serious with a gentleman, it is important to have an honest conversation with him, informing him of the things that matter to you and how you wish for him to treat you. In this case, chivalry. You would respectfully share that chivalry is very important to you. Make it clear to him that you value yourself, and it is important he values you as well. Not just in general, but in a way that speaks. Share with him your love language and get to know his love language as well. Let him know, without a doubt, that one of your love languages is being the recipient of chivalry.

Advise him that one of the things you would appreciate is if he is attentive enough to know when to seat you at the table wherever you are, in an informal or formal setting.

SEATING YOU AT THE TABLE

When my husband and I are in a restaurant or any other place we will sit, he knows when I stand near a chair, that is indication I wish to sit in that chair. He will then pull that chair out and seat me comfortably, then walk to his seat and seat himself. I don't have to say a word. He just knows. It is not because I demand it. He knows that I appreciate that type of treatment and being a recipient of chivalry is most definitely one of my love languages.

I have witnessed onlookers countless times because that deportment is so very rare. I've even had an elderly lady in a restaurant come to me, after witnessing my husband seat me, and say, "That is so very nice that he seated you." I giggled a bit and kindly stated, "Yes, thank you. He always seats me." It was a bit funny that she felt the need to share her observation with us, total strangers. At the time, I thought to myself, how sad that this act is done so rarely that once noticed, one feels the need to commend the person who exhibited the act and the recipient. Hence, the great need for chivalry and education on this topic.

Don't get me wrong; I would never say none of our guys demonstrate chivalry. However, many were not advised of these protocols. Many would gladly do it if they were respectfully taught the proper protocols. It is ok, ladies, to gently, with love, educate your guy on what matters to you in terms of chivalry and him seating you if he didn't demonstrate it on your first date.

Now, I don't recommend you demand it or say, "This is what you should do…" That's not a productive or constructive manner. He will have a defensive attitude, and it may not go well. Keep in mind, you are essentially informing him that he has to improve in an area, and he may feel as if you are attacking his manhood when you approach him that way. That is why you must choose your words carefully and deliver your request in kindness and love. Better yet, begin with a compliment. "You are such a wonderful man, and I appreciate you so much." Do not say "But" at this point. Simply continue by saying something like this, "Is it possible you can begin to be a little more chivalrous because it makes me feel so very special." Or you can say, "I would really love it if you would seat me whenever we are out. It would make me feel very special." If he cares about you and if he is truly a gentleman and perhaps was not privy to the chivalry concept, he will have no problem adjusting or discussing it further because he wants to make you feel like the special lady you are.

If you deliver your request in a loving way and he resists and it becomes problematic, then maybe you should rethink the direction you are going with him. However, there is nothing wrong with educating a gentleman about how you would like to be treated. Incidentally, be ready when he reciprocates and has requests of his own. This is a two-way street. It's about both in a relationship. So, don't go requesting if you are not prepared to deliver or adjust as well.

Let's discuss the protocols when being seated. The gentleman will place both hands on the back of the chair. He will pull the chair out far enough for you to comfortably stand in front of the chair. Once you stand in front of the chair, be sure the back of your knees touch the chair. He will then push the chair in gently, indicating to you to sit. Once you sit, place each hand on both sides of the chair. Remember, if you are wearing a skirt or dress, fold it under before sitting. After placing both hands on the side, you will then rise, and he will push the chair in just a bit more to have you closer to the table. Notice, I did not say once your hands are on the sides of the chair to assist you in rising, you then pull the chair. No, no, no! You only rise and ALLOW him to push the chair in a bit more. Try your very hardest to refrain from pulling the chair. Allow him to push the chair. Don't take away control. He is seating you. You should allow him to seat you. In this case, you want to give him full control to treat you the special way you like. Allow him to be chivalrous.

I invite you to view this video. **https://www.youtube.com/ watch?v=5zQjhr9smcY**

OPENING THE DOOR

When a gentleman opens the door for you, that is him being chivalrous. Considering everything mentioned in the previous section, it all applies to this as well.

Before entering a vehicle, it is important you walk to the door and step aside. This leaves way for the gentleman in your life to open the door for you. Once he opens the door, proceed with the protocols I mentioned in the entering and exiting a car section. He is treating you like the special lady you are. Enter the car like a lady as well. Once he closes your door, he then walks to his side and enters the car.

Keep in mind; this is whether or not you're the driver. Just because you're the driver doesn't mean he should not demonstrate chivalry.

Now, when he opens the door of a building, house, etc., he must stand on the outside to hold the door open. Once you enter, he enters after you and closes the door. It is crucial he doesn't open the door, then go inside to hold the door. He would remain out while holding the door. You may ask why he must hold it open while outside? It is because he is protecting you. If he goes inside, then he will leave you outdoors subjected to the elements of circumstance. So, no, he allows you in first, then he follows.

Remember, step aside, don't try to open the door. Get used to allowing the gentleman to be a gentleman. The keyword is ALLOW.

I invite you to view this video.
https://www.youtube.com/watch?v=widserxs3eQ

WHEN YOU AND YOUR GUY ARE DINING, ETC.

This is huge because, for some reason, there is confusion about this, and I'm just going to nip it in the bud right now. If he invites you to have a drink, breakfast, brunch, lunch, or dinner, he should be prepared to pay the tab. If you are on a date, he should be prepared to pay the tab. There is no ifs, ands, or buts about it. I am very old school and I believe in this etiquette protocol wholeheartedly. Now, if you all are just co-workers or just friends hanging out and decide to grab a bite to eat, you pay your own tab. That's called going "Dutch." If other arrangements are made prior, that's fine too.

However, if there is a relationship or a potential relationship and you are on a date, he should be prepared. If he is not prepared and pays his bill and looks to you to pay your bill, that's a good indication that you may need to have a conversation with him to voice your expectations as spelled out at the top of this chapter. Give him the benefit of the doubt because he may not know your expectations or the role of a gentleman. If he resists or gets upset because you respectfully shared expectations, you perhaps need to rethink the relationship or decide if you wish to continue pursuing a relationship with him. It's all up to you. However, I want to remind you that you are a lady, and if you lower your realistic standards in reference to the proper treatment by a man, you are essentially devaluing yourself.

On the other hand, he may invite you to have a drink, breakfast, lunch, etc., you can accept and propose that you both go Dutch, where he pays for his meal, and you pay for yours. You may choose to do this to prevent any level of expectations on either side. You may go further by proposing that you both drive separately. It is all up to you. Keep in mind that even though you propose to go Dutch, it doesn't mean you should not pay attention to whether he opens the door, pulls out your chair, etc.

Allow me to explain why I mentioned the latter part. A gentleman is a gentleman regardless if he is with his significant other, his mom, female cousin, auntie, or a female friend. A gentleman will open the door, pull out the chair, etc., for the lady in his presence. So, pay attention to those behaviors.

TIME TO PLACE THE ORDER

Once he has seated you and you are comfortable, the server will come to your table to take your order. A gentleman will allow the lady to order first. Even if the server goes to him first because the server was not educated on this protocol, he should inform the server to allow you to order first. Remember, chivalry enables the gentleman to ensure you are good and satisfied before he is. Therefore, he will have the server take your order first.

Now, I must say this. Just because you are first doesn't mean you should take an unreasonable amount of time to make your selection and place your order. Consider him and the fact that he may be hungry. Place your order as quickly as you can.

THE LAST PIECE OF HORS D'OEURVRES OR APPETIZER

Oh my Goodness! This protocol is a hidden fact that many of our gentlemen are not aware of and frankly, many ladies. So, let's briefly chat. It is considered a shared portion if you are on a date, and you've ordered hors d'oeuvres or appetizers for two. Let's say it is a serving of lemon pepper wings or some sort of dip and nachos. You're enjoying it so much. There is one piece or a small amount of serving left. The question is, who has first bids on that final piece or portion?

Well, as a gentleman, he would not eat it, having no concern whether or not you are satisfied. If he desires it, he will ask you, "Are you satisfied" or "Would you like the final portion?" at that point, you can say, "Yes, I would like it. Thank you." You can also say, "No, please, you enjoy it." Or you can say, "Why don't we share it?" I believe the most considerate thing to do is to say let's share it because that shows you are considering him as well as he is considering you.

HAT OR NO HAT

This protocol is often disregarded for some reason. Remind your guy to remove his hat when entering the restaurant or anywhere he will dine because it shows a sign of respect.

Remember, hats are considered outerwear for the gentleman, like a coat. It is polite to remove it upon entry.

It is not proper etiquette to sit at a table wearing a hat regardless of the style of the hat. Gentlemen should remove their hat.

Ladies are not called to remove their hat because it is generally a fashion statement with her attire. Traditionally, the hat was attached to her hair with a bobby pin and removing the hat would be impractical and certainly may cause her hair to be out of form. It is quite fine if she wears her hat indoors and in the restaurant.

No, it's not double standard. It's just the protocol.

LEAVING YOU BEHIND

A gentleman, in the spirit of chivalry, never walks and leaves the lady behind. He walks alongside her. Now, keep in mind, these protocols are typically practiced in the American culture. In many other cultures, it is customary for the lady to walk behind the man. However, in the American culture, the couple walks together, or the gentleman allows the lady to walk in front of him. Of course, there are times she falls behind to speak with someone privately or have a conversation with a friend. He would either join her or allow them to converse. Once they resume walking together, he must be aware of her position and fall into the protocol.

If your guy is walking ahead of you and leaving you behind to fend for yourself, you may want to speak with him kindly about that.

THE STAIRS AND ELEVATOR

This is pretty basic, however, one that needs to be mentioned. When you and your guy are going into the elevator, he allows you in first. When exiting, he allows you to exit first.

When going up the stairs, he allows you up first. Awwe, but there's a twist. When going down the stairs, he goes down first. Because he is always looking for opportunities to demonstrate chivalry, he will realize that there is potential danger. You can possibly fall down the stairs, especially if you're wearing heels. Therefore, as your protector, he will be a step or two in front of you just in case you fall, he will break your fall. You will fall on him to cushion your fall. He will do this to ensure you are not hurt if you were to fall. Isn't that so sweet?

WHO WALKS WHERE AND WHEN?

Speaking of walking. Keeping in mind that the chivalrous thing to do is to protect the lady in his presence, a gentleman walks along the side of the traffic when walking down the street. He does this to protect you. Again, there is potential danger. He sees you can possibly be stricken by a vehicle. Of course, we certainly don't wish for him to be stricken either. However, if he is on the side of the traffic, he will have the ability to protect you by perhaps pushing you over to safety. Now, God forbid, there is a puddle, and a car drives in the puddle, and there is a splash, there is a great chance he will receive the brunt of the water. Eewww! LOL I know, gross, right? But it happens. He will protect you.

I want you to go a little further. Even when you are walking down the lane of a store's parking lot, he should still walk on the side of the traffic, and you walk on the side of the parked cars or alongside the building.

I can tell you that my husband understands that concept because wherever we go, he ensures I am on the inside, and he is in his protective position.

It is not to say you are weak or you have given away your independence. Please don't perceive it that way. As a lady in a relationship, you must demonstrate to that gentleman that he is needed and desired. One of the ways to do that, is to allow him to exhibit chivalry if that is what you require.

Now, understand that it is not just some guys that may not know the chivalry protocols. Many women and young ladies have also not grasped the concept of allowing a gentleman to treat her like the queen or special lady she truly is. In this case, I encourage you to let go and allow yourself to be treated with dignity, respect, and gentleness by that gentleman. Again, notice the words gentle and man.

So, if you are in a relationship and have not yet embraced the concept of your guy being chivalrous toward you, perhaps having a conversation in that regard may be a good thing to do. At the end of the day, though, it is your choice. After reading this information, I hope you will be more open to accepting this type of wonderful treatment from the right guy.

Before we leave this section, I want to make very clear that if this guy is not treating you properly in other instances and is not respecting you in other instances, then that is when you must rethink and consider what is needed to improve the relationship or assist him in improving, if you desire. He may be a master at chivalry and harms you in other ways. That, for sure, is not acceptable. Please take what I am sharing with you into perspective. If you are being abused or harmed, take proper measures to ensure your safety and maintenance of your confidence and self-love.

Now, besides that significant other, understand chivalry can be exhibited by your son, dad, brother, male cousin, nephew, grandad, etc. It doesn't have to only be done by your significant other.

GENTLE REMINDER GENTLEMEN

In the corporate environment, chivalry is frowned upon because women desire to be treated equally. They do not wish to be considered the weaker party or one who needs to be cared for. Therefore, chivalry is scarce in corporate spaces. However, don't confuse that with courtesy. It is still courteous to hold a door open for the person behind you or say, "No, you go ahead." That may not be particularly chivalrous. It's being courteous. Know what I mean?

If a gentleman is determined to be chivalrous in the workplace, he must be extremely careful because it can be misconstrued as sexual harassment or discrimination. It's a thin line. I recommend that gentlemen make every effort to understand the culture of his workplace to be sure his deportment is consistent with the culture. He wants to be appropriate and not offend or cause awkward circumstances. Focus on being courteous, which is expected from everyone, male or female.

CHAPTER 11
TABLE ETIQUETTE & PROTOCOL

This subject is rather broad because there are many protocols, and I am excited to get into it step by step.

Table Etiquette is a skill that much of our population are unsure about. Because of their uncertainty, many do not practice it. As I teach this subject, I am alarmingly made aware of the great number of children and adults who either find it challenging to demonstrate proper table etiquette or were never taught. In many cases, it is not their fault. One of the reasons I teach these protocols is to help them understand that proper table etiquette is attractive and certainly catches attention, good attention.

We are going to remain consistent and pretend you are in a restaurant. Let's say you're in a five-star restaurant, a high-end restaurant, where table etiquette is expected, and the staff is familiar with the protocols for the most part. In a five-star restaurant, the service, and the food are expected to be superb. The ambiance is inviting and the environment is one in which you feel comfortable. In addition, remember, the restaurant is rated five stars.

Now, I can share with you that there is one seven-star restaurant in the world that I know of, and it is in Dubai, called Burj Al Arab Jumeirah. Are you surprised? LOL Dubai is breathtaking! I would like to experience dining there one day. For now, I will enjoy the exquisite restaurants within the states and other countries I visit.

I absolutely love visiting fine restaurants because of the service, and typically, everyone takes pride in the total operation of the restaurant, from the host to the chef.

HOST * WAITER * WAITRESS

When you enter most restaurants, there is typically someone at the front. They will ask you how many are in your party or ask if you have reservations. That individual is considered the host (male) or hostess (female). They are responsible for greeting guests. A very important aspect of their duty is to greet you with a smile and make you feel welcomed.

The host, in many cases, will seat you and provide a menu. There are some restaurants where the host will beckon a server to escort you to your table and provide the menu at that point. The host is the first and typically, the last impression of the establishment. They greet you and, more than likely, on your way out, will say, "It was a pleasure to have you, enjoy your day" or something like that.

Keep in mind in upscale restaurants, you will more than likely have also a maître d'. A maître d' ensures that the guests receive top-notch service. He/she greets the guest and sometimes even gives them a handshake or an alternative to a handshake before they begin to dine.

The maître d' also ensures that the service flows and there is no longer than normal wait or awkwardness for the guests. They supervise the servers. If the maître d' realizes the order is taking a bit longer than normal to arrive, he/she will visit your table and perhaps offer a drink on the house. During your dining experience, the maître d' will also stop by the table and ask if you are enjoying your meal. By the way, the waiter or waitress will do that as well. The maître d' and server have one job, to ensure the guests have a top-notch experience and gives them great ratings and reviews. That is how the establishment maintains its five-star or higher status.

WAITER * WAITRESS

Before we get into this aspect, it is important to know that the waiter is the male, and the waitress is the female. I felt the need to mention that because in any given restaurant, I've heard guests addressing female servers as waiter, which is neither appropriate nor correct. That can certainly be offensive. Now, because she may value you as a guest and wishes to deliver acceptable customer service, she will not correct you. Nonetheless, I am sure she may be offended when addressed as a man.

So, be very aware of how you beckon or address the waiter or waitress. When I dine in restaurants, I make it a point to ask the server's first name if they are not wearing a badge. If they are wearing a badge, I take the time to notice the name and address them by their name on the badge. That leads to better interactions and causes them to feel that you see them as a person and not just someone serving. You have to agree that everyone loves to hear their name, especially when there are opportunities and great interactions. You can't deny that.

TIME TO BE SERVED

When the server arrives to serve your food, whether it be a waiter or waitress, a well-versed server knows to serve on the left and collect on the right.

This is an important protocol. This leads to the prevention of the server reaching over you to retrieve an item or to serve a dish.

I've been in restaurants that are not necessarily five-star and have witnessed and been victim of the server literally reaching over me to serve another guest. Mind you, he/she could've walked around to the other person. However, to take a shortcut, they reach over my plate and extend their arms to place the dish in front of the guest beside me. That is most annoying to me because it is clear they just don't wish to make a couple of steps to properly deliver the dish.

I have found it to be overbearing when it is done repeatedly. I have had to ask the server respectfully and tactfully to please walk around to the guest and serve them. The response I often receive is, "Oh, I'm sorry, no problem." I then say to myself, "Wow!"

So, understand every server doesn't know this protocol. Unless you are dining in an upscale restaurant, these protocols are not always practiced. I must tell you though, when you are served on the wrong side, don't become upset. No need to correct them because they just don't know. However, if they reach over your food or reach over you, I recommend you nip that in the bud with poise and kindness.

There are exceptions in terms of reaching over. If you are sitting in a booth, then the server can't walk to the neighboring guests.

Therefore, I will assist the server by taking the dish and handing it to the guest next to me to prevent the server from reaching over my dish. It then becomes a collaborative effort.

ADDITIONAL STAFF MEMBERS

In any given restaurant, there are a host of employees playing different roles with different duties. A typical guest will interact with the host, waiter or waitress, busser, and headwaiter. As I mentioned before, high-end restaurants typically have a maître d'. Let's understand the essential duties of each.

BUSSER

A busser has a very important task. Without bussers, a restaurant will not flow as efficiently as it should. Bussers set tables. When guests have finished dining, they remove the items and clean the table. He or she may also serve the guest water and sometimes deliver the basket or serving of bread before the waiter or waitress arrives to take the order.

We appreciate bussers because their role helps ensure that guests will have a great experience in the restaurant.

HEADWAITER

A headwaiter typically supervises the whole operation of the dining room where they work. The head waiter can also be referred to as the maître d'. They carry essentially the same duties.

BARTENDER

A bartender's job is crucial as well because he/she prepares the drinks for the guests. Keep in mind, a bartender doesn't only prepare alcoholic beverages. He/she also prepares mixed non-alcoholic drinks, juices, soft drinks (sodas), etc. Whatever the guests order as a beverage, except coffee or tea, comes from the bartender.

So, let's dispel that myth that bartenders only prepare alcoholic beverages.

The bartender's duty is to maintain inventory at the bar and ensure they do not run out of the items that allow them to prepare the drinks on the menu. The last thing a credible restaurant wants is for the guest to order a drink they say they serve on the menu, and the server or bartender must inform the guests that they are out of it. Not good! Therefore, maintaining inventory is crucial.

CHEF

Finally, the most important staff member, a chef. There's no eating without him/her. What is a restaurant without the chef?

They prepare the meal. Hopefully, you enjoy the meal. They remain in the kitchen through their shift pouring their talents and expertise into the meals with hopes everything is delicious, and you rave about it.

If you ever think about it, you will realize that the person who completes the whole experience, the chef, never gets to see the smiles on people's faces when they are full and satisfied. They don't get to hear when the server comes around and asks you how your food is, and you reply by telling them, it's great. They don't hear that.

Here is something I highly recommend. When you enjoy the food, send a little note to the chef saying thank you and briefly share that you enjoyed their dish or dishes. In addition, it is ok to give gratuity to the chef as well as the server.

I would never say, remember the "Little man" in the back because the chef is no little man or woman. His or her role is significant.

So, the next time you have a great dining experience in a restaurant, try not to only compliment the server but also compliment the chef. I hope that makes sense to you. Incidentally, if you are invited to a private dining party, be sure to compliment the chef of that event as well. It's just the proper thing to do.

Those are the typical staff members in a restaurant in addition to the maître d' and headwaiter that are usually in upscale restaurants and the dining room of cruise ships.

DINING-VS-EATING

If you're honest with yourself, most of the time, when you wish to head to a restaurant, or you are inviting someone to a restaurant, you would say something like, "Let's eat at…" or "Let's go to… to eat."

There is a very big distinction between dining and eating. Don't be alarmed if you're a bit confused because I didn't know either until I learned. So, don't feel bad.

When you visit a restaurant, especially an upscale restaurant, you want to have a dining experience rather than just eat.

Allow me to explain the difference.

When someone has a dining experience, this is typically what they do to ensure they have an experience and not just eat. They will:

- Enjoy the ambiance of the room. The ambiance helps set the tone and the mood of the guests—the overall atmosphere in the restaurant.
- Enjoy the beautification of the table. In most upscale restaurants, the table is set so very nicely with the silverware or flatware, chargers in some cases, centerpiece, tablecloth, and any other item that may be on the table to accentuate.
- Enjoy the other guests at the table by having great conversations, laughing gracefully, and having a wonderful time.
- Most importantly, you enjoy the meal served, one course at a time. That is when you take the time to taste the food, savor it, and just enjoy your portions.
- Of course, you demonstrate table etiquette and enjoy doing so.
- Finally, you enjoy your interaction with the servers. When they offer you something you don't desire, you wouldn't just say, "No", you would say "No, thank you". If you desire it, you would say, "Yes, thank you." Thank yous, and all the niceties that go along with courteous interaction are a part of having a pleasant experience. Don't forget to smile.

EATING

When you visit a restaurant to eat:
- You are only concerned about consuming the food on your plate.
- Your focus is only on what's in front of you.
- Table Etiquette is the last thing on your mind.
- You just want to eat.
- You may have a little conversation while eating.
- You are not concerned about having an experience and savoring the taste.

Therefore, when visiting a restaurant, we should have a mindset to have an experience. So, the next time you wish to invite someone out or inform someone you would like to dine in a restaurant, think about saying something like this, "Let's dine at…" or "I'm going to…to dine."

Now, there are times you may visit a restaurant and just eat if you're in a hurry or when under other circumstances. However, it is important that I share the difference with you to allow you to be more interested in having experiences, rather than just visiting the restaurant to eat. Sometimes, we truly need to slow down and take the time to have an experience. Take the time to be present.

I hope that helps. It all boils down to being refined and taking the time to demonstrate the protocols and enjoy the benefits of being refined. By the way, you certainly can dine at home as well. Enjoy!

SEATING YOURSELF IN THE RESTAURANT

I'm sure there will be times you visit a restaurant by yourself to have that quiet and alone time. I do it often, especially for lunch. I sometimes need to clear my mind and just ponder on things over a delicious meal.

Of course, you won't have a gentleman with you to seat you. If you are being served by a waiter (male), allow him to seat you if he offers because every waiter is not necessarily aware of that protocol. If you are not served by a waiter, seat yourself. However, be sure to sit gracefully and not just drop your body. That, too, is noticed.

INDEX FINGER & NAPKIN ETIQUETTE

We have two index fingers, and we sometimes don't know the power of the index fingers when dining. They control the napkin and the utensils.

Let's first discuss the napkin and how the index finger holds the napkin. Keep in mind it is not proper etiquette to wipe your mouth with a napkin. I know you're like, "Whatttt???" LOL No, we don't wipe our mouth. We dab our mouth. Male or female, it is not proper to wipe your mouth. Dabbing is not a feminine thing; it is the proper protocol.

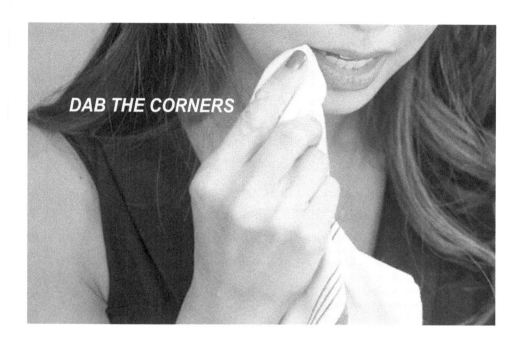

DAB THE CORNERS

When you are seated, you want to be sure to place your napkin on your lap. If you are having breakfast, lunch, or tea, the napkin is generally smaller, depending on where you are. The napkin would be fully unfolded and placed on your lap. You may wonder why it may be smaller. Typically, breakfast and lunch are smaller portions in the American culture. The napkin need not be so large. So, it is appropriate to lay it unfolded on your lap.

If you are having dinner, the napkin will typically be larger because it is common that dinner is a larger portion, again in the American culture. In this case, you would not lay the napkin fully unfolded on your lap, you would fold the napkin in half. Lay it on your lap with the folded side facing your abdomen.

Remember, while dining, your napkin always goes on your lap. It is not a bib. Therefore, it should not be placed in your shirt below your mouth. After all, you are preparing to have a dining experience. It would look quite awkward having your napkin hanging from your shirt.

Don't hang your napkin on the back of the chair either if you must leave to return.

Here is something that's going to perhaps cause you to ask why. If the napkin or anything for that matter falls to the floor, DO NOT pick it up. I know it is a natural reflex to immediately pick something up that has fallen. However, in this case, there is an exception. It is grossly improper to pick something up from the floor while dining, especially if dining with others. You don't want to transfer the germs from the floor to the table. That's not sanitary and it can cause a guest to lose their appetite or just feel awkward.

Simply leave the item on the floor. Once your server comes to your table, or you gracefully signal them because they are close to your table, simply say something like this, "I'm sorry, I dropped my napkin. May I have another one, please?" Their response will always be "Sure," and they will pick it up and replenish it. Remember, it is a part of their duty, and they are ok with it as long as you ask respectfully. When interacting with your server, always, and I mean always, be courteous, respectful, and polite because they are simply working to take care of themselves and their family. They deserve respect.

Remember in the early read of this book, I reminded you that no one is any better than you and you are no better than anyone? With that in mind, we must all respect each other, whether it be the server, busser, or CEO.

114

If a server shows you disrespect, then you should not stoop to their level, which may cause a scene. Simply inform their superior, and hopefully, they will reprimand the server and apologize to you for the less than great experience you had. Who knows, you may end up with a free meal. LOL

UNTIMELY BODILY FUNCTIONS

There are bodily functions you may be unable to control, and there are some you can, while dining. What I'm about to share with you is extremely important as you develop into a refined individual. Regardless of the bodily function, your delivery of the following is of utmost importance. Your execution must be done in such a way that it doesn't offend the other guests. You certainly don't want to be the one to cause someone to lose their appetite or, even worse, want to leave. Let's discuss them.

BURPING

Burping is a bodily function that is, for the most part, uncontrollable, especially after you have taken a drink of any beverage. The question is, should it be done at the table? Well, considering it is an involuntary bodily function, you really don't have a say. LOL If you are dining with others and you feel that a burp is about to take place, simply turn away from the other guests, cover your mouth with your napkin, CLOSE YOUR MOUTH, then go ahead and release that inner burp in a way that makes it almost impossible to hear. Now, if your burp is heard, simply acknowledge it, say, "Excuse me, I'm so sorry," with a light giggle, and carry on to another subject or continue enjoying your food. Do not dwell on it because it can become a very awkward conversation and is not an appropriate topic to be discussed in that setting.

Everyone knows burping is involuntary. The trick is releasing it so that it lessens the sound and you do not make a scene.

COUGHING & SNEEZING

Coughing and sneezing are other bodily functions that are involuntary as well, and will come when you least expect them. Whether you're dining or not, it is never good to cough or sneeze anywhere on your hand or in your palms. That is extremely inappropriate, especially when you are dining with others.

If you were to cough or sneeze in your hands, your germs will be in or on your hands, whether you see it or not. While dining, it is expected, at times, that you hand dishes to others or pitchers of water or drinks to someone. When you sneeze or cough in your hands and hand things to others, you are essentially spreading your germs and everything that comes with the germs to the other guests. Even if you're not dining, coughing, and sneezing in or on your hands, spread germs when you touch doorknobs, hand items to someone, shake someone's hand, just to name a few. There are countless ways to spread your germs just by coughing and or sneezing in your hands.

If you feel a need to cough or sneeze, simply turn to your left or right, away from your neighbor, and cough or sneeze in your elbow. The objective is to ensure the germs or fluids go into your elbow's crease and not on a napkin or in your hand.

Please do not take your napkin and cough or sneeze in it. More than likely, at some point in dining, your napkin will end up on the table, and we certainly do not want the germs there.

When you turn to the right or left, aim your elbow downward pointing to the floor. As you sneeze or cough in your elbow, whatever exits your system will go down toward the floor or in your elbow for the most part and will not go directly across to anyone. This protocol is crucial, especially when dining or when near someone.

BLOWING THE NOSE

Remember, I mentioned burping, coughing, and sneezing are involuntary bodily functions. Well, blowing your nose is not involuntary. You control the timing of that. Blowing your nose at the table is inexcusable, unacceptable, improper etiquette, offensive, and indeed graphic.

Under no circumstances should you ever blow your nose at the table. NOOOOOOO!

I cannot tell you how many times I have dined in restaurants, and someone sitting at the table across from me or in my sight blows their nose. Get this, the worst part is that they typically blow their nose with the fabric napkin provided by the restaurant. Then, hold on, it gets worse. They place the napkin on the plate or on the table for the server to collect.

That is one of the most inconsiderate acts anyone can do in a restaurant. So, because the server has picked up the same napkin to take to the kitchen to be washed, they may have transferred their germs to the server or anyone else who touched that napkin. That is the epitome of improper etiquette and certainly inappropriate.

Here is what you do when you feel you need to blow your nose. Simply excuse yourself. Please don't announce that you need to blow your nose. The graphic mental image is not what you wish to give the other guests. So, simply excuse yourself, go to the restroom, blow your nose, wash your hands, return to the table refreshed, and carry on with an unrelated topic. Blowing your nose is not a topic to discuss or anything that has to do with it.

You will know you need to blow your nose when you begin to sniffle. Don't keep doing that. Head to the restroom to take care of that. Ok! If you have a bad cold or constant runny nose, maybe you should forgo the visit to the restaurant for that time. Just maybe…

CHEWING DO'S AND DON'T

As a child, I have always heard, chew with your mouth closed. Don't chew with your mouth open. While dining, it can be tempting to chew with your mouth open at times. It is certainly not proper etiquette to chew with your mouth open. The other guests are certainly not interested in seeing the mushy food in your mouth. That's not pleasant at all.

When chewing, simply close your lips and continue chewing. It's not rocket science. Close your lips and chew. When you do that, you certainly look more polished and disciplined as one who is concerned about their deportment at the table.

Incidentally, if someone asks you a question or says something that requires a response, politely hold up your index finger, indicating to them to hold on just a moment, smile, and continue chewing. Once you are finished chewing and consuming that portion, you may proceed with the response. Take your time, be patient, and always be concerned about your conduct and how it will be perceived at your table. This is not just for when you're in a restaurant. It is while dining anywhere, home, a friend's, grandma's, auntie's, etc. It doesn't matter. Proper table etiquette is always a good thing, and it makes you shine in the experience. It also boosts your confidence that you can effectively function in this environment without making an obvious faux pas (embarrassing act in a social situation).

FINGER LICKING GOOD

I know this protocol violation is so very common, it makes me giggle. Sometimes you will eat something that is super delicious, and it gets all over your fingers because it's finger food, and you succumb to temptation and go to licking those fingers.

STOP RIGHT THERE! You should not lick your fingers. Nooooo! LOL It is certainly not proper etiquette to lick fingers regardless of how delicious the food or sauce may taste. I really like wings, and we know wings are finger food, just as sandwiches, pizza slices, fries, etc. When I am enjoying my wings, depending on the flavor wings: barbeque, blue cheese dressing, or any other flavor, I can be tempted because the sauce is on my fingers, and I just want to get it all. This is when my table etiquette skills kick in even more. I encourage you to take that napkin and wipe your fingers. Yes, all that sauce is gone into the napkin and not in your mouth. It's quite ok to wipe with the napkin and not lick your fingers. It says you are refined, poised, polished, and you are concerned about your conduct.

Therefore, when you take a plate or are served a plate, you ensure that you have a napkin on your lap, and it is readily accessible when you need it. Every time you dine, whether at home or anywhere else, always be sure you possess a napkin. If you need another napkin, don't be afraid to politely request one.

ELBOWS OR NO ELBOWS

No elbows on the table, please. That's table etiquette 101. You've probably heard this all through your childhood, "No elbows on the table, no elbows on the table." There is a reason, while dining, you should not have your elbows on the table. Picture this, generally, you have your entire setting at your placement, and the outer perimeters of your plate would be your utensils. The utensils mark the end of your perimeter unless you are having tea where there will be a teacup and saucer on the upper right of your knife and spoon, for example. Now, if you were to place your elbows on the table, that would likely mean your elbows will be outside of your perimeter, encroaching on someone else's perimeter. There are several boundaries when dining, that is one of them. Not only that, your body parts should not be rested on the table either. We should be sitting up with proper posture, not using the table to rest our body.

Surprisingly, there is a time when it is permissible to place your elbows on the table. This is before or after your meal. If there is food on the table or if even one person is still enjoying their food, your elbows should not be on the table; that is rude.

If all guests are finished, and the plates, etc., have been taken, and everyone is just conversing and spending even more quality time together, at that point, it is appropriate to place your elbows on the table within your perimeter.

Allow me to also explain why elbows land on the table. More than likely, your posture is not upright. Proper posture, as you know, is extremely important, especially at the table. Now, when you sit at the table and do not have proper posture, it is natural to look for the support of the table. You are not allowing your back muscles to support you sitting upright. You are allowing the table to keep you up.

On the other hand, if you were to sit upright (erect), you would not seek support because you will allow your back to support you. See what I mean? So, please sit up straight, buttocks pushed to the back of the chair, roll shoulders back, then drop them, and enjoy your experience demonstrating proper posture throughout.

PACE YOURSELF

When dining, it is very common to have multiple courses. It could be Soup, Salad, Sorbet, Entrée, and Dessert, that is a typical American five-course meal in an upscale restaurant. A typical European five-course meal would be hors d'oeuvre, appetizer, salad, entrée, and dessert. Very similar to the American culture. However, because their portions may be smaller, they can have even more courses. Everything in etiquette and protocol differ depending on the culture.

First, when you arrive at your table, you sit after your host sits. You don't want to sit unless the host has sat or has beckoned you to sit while they do something else.

Once your first course is served, it is improper etiquette to begin enjoying your food before everyone at the table has received their first course. Once everyone at your immediate table has received their course, then you proceed along with everyone else, enjoying your course. If you are at a private dinner party, once the host or hostess sits and picks up their utensil(s), you may proceed and enjoy your course. It is essential to eat at a moderate and reasonable pace to ensure you finish the course nearly or at the same time as everyone else, keeping in mind that if just one person is enjoying any particular course, a well-versed server, will not serve the next course. That simply means the other guests will be waiting for you to receive their next course.

That said, be considerate of other guests. If it takes you forever to complete your meal at home, you must make a considerate adjustment when dining out with others. If you're alone in a restaurant, enjoy yourself and take a little longer than you would if you were with guests. However, consider that any given server does not wish to serve a guest for an extremely long time because that limits the gratuity they would receive for the day and there may be other guests that could be seated at the table where you are.

I truly hope by now you have grasped the concept of etiquette. Keep in mind; it is not always about self, it is about how your deportment impacts and affects others in your presence or, sometimes, indirectly. **It's civility (politeness and courtesy toward others).**

PASS THE STRING BEANS, PLEASE

When dining, it is common to pass dishes. I alluded to this earlier in this read. It is important never to reach over another guest's food. Nor is it proper to shout, "Pass the string beans, please." It is not appropriate to get up and walk over and reach for the string beans or anything you desire on the table.

You simply ask, "May I have the string beans, please?" You would not say, "Can I...", you would say, "May I...", which is most appropriate.

Once you have made your request, the guest who sits closest to the item will reach for it without reaching over anyone, and if you are at a distance, pass it around until it gets to you.

WHICH DIRECTION TO PASS

When passing a dish, it is most appropriate to pass a dish or anything to the right. You do not pass to the left when someone is at a distance from you. If someone is at your immediate left, right next to you, you may hand it to them. If they are at a distance, simply hand it to the person on your right, they will hand it to the right to the next person, and that person will hand it to the next person until it reaches the guest who requested it.

Here is a catch, though. You know how at times you are dining with others and a dish is passed, headed to the guest who requested it, and you say, "Oh, I'd like some" and you take a portion, so does the next person and the next? If everyone does that, there will perhaps be a very small portion, or none left for the person who requested it because those who sat between them and the initial person who began passing it have taken a portion. That is certainly not proper etiquette.

Proper protocol suggests that you allow the person who has requested it to receive it and take their portion. If you would like a portion, make your request and it will be handed to you. Incidentally, the person who initiates the passing should not take a portion either. Pass it on to the guest who requested it first. Please be mindful of this protocol.

SALT AND PEPPER PROTOCOL

This is a little-known fact. Just about everyone I've enlightened on this protocol had no idea, prior.

Salt and pepper are never separated. If some request the salt during their dining experience, they receive the pepper as well. It is proper protocol to keep them together. If someone requests the pepper, they will receive the salt as well.

Now, keep in mind, more than likely, someone will ask why you are passing both. That is a wonderful teaching opportunity when you kindly inform them that it is proper etiquette to hand both together.

I like to say they are married. You definitely don't want to separate married folks. You may say some need to be separated. LOL However, that's not the topic. LOL

So, one would not go without the other. This is a little-known fact that needs to become well known when dining.

UTENSILS

This is simple and precise. Do not place a used utensil back onto the table. If you have used a utensil, keep it on your plate or in your bowl or the plate that accompanied the bowl. Please don't place it on the table.

It is typical for me to visit different countries and experience different cultures. Can you imagine if I visit Italy and purchased a beautiful handmade tablecloth? I decide to have a private dinner and the theme is Italian. You're enjoying the delicious pasta and sauce, and once you're finished with your course, you place your utensils directly on the tablecloth. Nooooo! You just ruined my tablecloth that clearly, I cannot replace. That is certainly inappropriate. For so many other reasons, used utensils should not even be tilted on the table. Please leave your used utensils in the plate or bowl to be collected to prevent incidents.

BREAK OR CUT THE BREAD?

Before enjoying your delicious meal, it is customary that most restaurants provide rolls or a warm slice of specialty bread for you to enjoy until your first course is served. Enjoy your bread or roll.

However, you do not want to cut the bread. Nope, you want to break the bread. You would break a small piece. I like to say, break one morsel at a time and enjoy it. Remember, to break a moderate amount to gracefully place in your mouth. I know you may be used to breaking or cutting the roll in half and buttering the entire half and biting from it. That's not the proper protocol.

Once you place the bread on your bread plate or a server places it there for you, simply break a piece from the corner, butter or spread preserve on it, then enjoy it. You would repeat this process until the bread is finished or you've had enough.

While dining in a formal or informal setting, this is the only time your hands should touch your food unless the other foods are finger foods. It is permissible and appropriate to break your bread with your hands.

If there is a basket or a serving of rolls/bread on the table for everyone, you may proceed by taking your bread, making sure your fingers or nothing personal touches the other pieces. After you have taken your bread, offer it to the guest sitting on your right. Don't just take the bread and place it back on the table. We want to always consider that someone else may desire a serving as well.

So, the next time you are served bread, try to remember these etiquette protocols.

SPILLAGE

Let's continue discussing protocols at the table. As you can see, there are so many different protocols that lend to a pleasant dining experience and assist you in conducting yourself in an appropriate manner.

Because we are all human and mistakes happen, there may be a time or two when you spill your water or any other beverage onto the table. It is extremely important at this time to refrain from making a scene. Yes, attempt to clean up the spillage. However, if you cannot clean the spillage with just your napkin, then you will need the assistance of the server. I highly recommend not asking the other guests at your table to give you their napkins. That is not appropriate. Simply request assistance from the server, and they will assist you. They are always available to you, so don't make a scene grabbing everyone's napkin and trying to clean it yourself.

Now, here is something very important, while the server is cleaning the spillage, sit back and remain that way until the server has cleaned the area properly. Essentially, you want to stay out of their way and allow them to complete the task. Don't be hard on yourself because you spilled something. You're human, we all make mistakes. However, what we do next is what matters and can determine in which direction the experience will go.

CONVERSATIONS AT THE TABLE

As you enjoy a great dining experience, remember, one word, one statement, one reference can cause everything to go left at the table. Therefore, you must be cognizant of the topic you choose to raise or refer to.

They always say, don't discuss religion or politics because they are such controversial topics. Now, if everyone is of the same faith or belief in politics, then the conversation may be quite interesting and healthy.

In addition, it all depends on the caliber of individuals at the table. Some folks just cannot respect the opinion of others and will become upset if a statement is made or thought expressed that is contrary to theirs or may even feel threatened. Therefore, avoid any subject that may create that atmosphere or trigger such emotions.

I recommend, to be safe, you discuss topics that don't have the potential to cause discomfort, awkwardness or such upset that will cause someone to leave.

Converse on topics that will not induce hostile or negative emotions or expressions. Don't speak on something that may seem disrespectful to a guest, and certainly don't throw anyone under the bus by speaking their business at the table.

Remember, the goal is for everyone to have a pleasant dining experience. They should begin and end with a pleasant smile. Now, of course, there are times when serious and tough topics must be discussed in a private setting. However, not in a general social setting, not at Thanksgiving dinner, and not at Christmas dinner. I think you get the picture, right?

As you dine with others, know it is a **NO CELL PHONE ZONE**. That is not the time to have a cell phone in your hand and a fork in the other. It is ok to leave your cell phone in your purse, in your pocket, or anywhere other than your hand and on the table.

This is the time to get to know each other or just have pleasant conversations.

When you sit at the table speaking with someone on the phone or texting, you are sending the message to the other guests that they are not important enough and that the person you are texting or speaking with is more important. That is the message it sends. Using a cell phone at the table in an isolated manner is:

- Rude
- Improper etiquette
- Can be offensive
- Inconsiderate of the other guests at the table

Take the opportunity to:

- Converse with the guests.
- Ask them how their day was.
- Tell them about your day.
- Share ideas.
- Get to know them even more.

If a cell phone is used while dining, it is recommended that it is only when everyone has agreed to utilize it to take pictures of the food, group selfie, or frontal picture of the group. It certainly doesn't appear respectful when used for an isolated occurrence. So, be sure if it is out, everyone is involved. That's the right thing to do, and that is proper etiquette.

When setting the table, there is no place for a cell phone if you think about it. With that said, I highly recommend you leave the cell phone out of sight, sending a message to the other guests that you are present with them. This is even more important when dining with family, including your children. It is equally important to teach our children that cell phones should not be used at the table except for emergency purposes. This must be emphasized because at any given time you visit a restaurant, you may see a family around a table, and mom, dad, and children are on their phones. The question is, who is talking with who? That time is a great opportunity for everyone to be present and learn more about each other and give their undivided attention. That attention should not be divided between those in your presence and someone on the phone. I know it's tempting. Just think about it for me. Being present is so very important. By the way, the same protocol applies when having dinner with family at home.

There was a time I would go out with my husband, and once I sat, I would pull out my phone. I thought it was an opportunity to focus on a text, surf the net or social media, or make a call.

After becoming an Etiquette Consultant and learning the importance of this protocol, I understand the message it sends, and I most definitely stopped. My husband recognizes that I no longer utilize my phone, and he takes the opportunity to converse on different topics, and I truly enjoy it. Before that, he would humbly wait until I finished using the phone, to speak. Sadly, because of my lack of etiquette, at the time, I did not consider the message I sent him. Clearly, unconsciously I disregarded the fact that we were there to spend quality time. Don't get me wrong, I respect my husband. I love him so very much and I love spending time with him. I just always thought it was ok to pull out the phone. I did not consider the message it sent. So, always think about the message when you pick up the phone instead of conversing with the person or persons at your table.

Now, I know there are times for emergency calls. We are not referring to circumstances such as those. We are referring to the fundamentals of dining with others and the cell phone, the great distractor.

CLINK GLASSES OR NO?

Tradition is a powerful thing. Traditionally, when giving a toast, everyone clinks glasses or knocks glasses to complete the toast. However, that is not correct. I'm so sorry to burst your bubble.

It is improper etiquette to clink glasses. It makes noise, and it certainly isn't graceful. Even if you see others doing it, you know it is improper, so I highly recommend you refrain from doing it now that you are aware of that protocol.

Here's a twist to this topic. If you are dining or drinking with your significant other, it is permitted to clink glasses between the two of you. Otherwise, no clinking.

TOAST TO YOU

When giving a toast, it is proper to simply raise the glass toward the person honored or to the host. Raising your glass and saying "Cheers" is sufficient and very appropriate.

If the toast is to you, you do not drink in your honor. Allow the other guests to drink in your honor. Do not stand in your honor either. Once everyone is seated, you may stand and express your gratitude.

Typically, when giving a toast in a group, the guests have in hand a stem glass. When holding a stem glass, it is important to hold only the stem of the glass and not the bowl of the glass. If you hold the bowl of the glass with the beverage in it, your hand may warm the beverage, and we certainly don't want to change the temperature of the beverage unless it is your intention. When holding the stem, you would hold it toward the ends of your fingers. You would not fully place your hand around the stem as if you were coddling the stem.

WHEN ENJOYING YOUR DRINK

As we discuss drinking, I want to remind you of the importance of remaining graceful as a lady or gentleman when drinking from a glass or cup.

When drinking, you must look into the glass, this may seem weird. You're probably wondering, why am I looking at the beverage? Well, you look into the glass to pay attention to the flow of the beverage to prevent it from spilling on you, or at the corners of your mouth or worse choking you, because you poured too much in your mouth.

I must be honest, back in the day when I would drink, I would not pay attention to the flow of anything. LOL I would be laughing or getting a sip in between words, and there have been times, the beverage has spilled or even run down the sides of my mouth or worse because I poured too much into my mouth, I nearly choked. Yeah, that's because I wasn't paying attention.

Therefore, when you are drinking, take the time to look into your glass or cup and be sure the flow of the beverage is moderate, and there is little or no chance of spillage or any other faux pas.

In addition to that, if you are wearing lipstick and realize after taking a drink that the lipstick has made an imprint on the rim of the glass or cup, please be sure to drink from the same area. You certainly do not wish to have lipstick marks all around the rim. That certainly isn't proper etiquette, and it certainly isn't something a polished lady would consciously do. So, please be cognizant of where your lipstick imprints and remain in that area. This, of course, will contribute to you being more refined.

SORBET HMMMM GOOD!

As we enjoy our meal, especially in upscale restaurants, it is good to order "Sorbet" to cleanse our palates.

Let's discuss this fabulous course that many may not be aware of. Sorbet is a French word. Keep in mind; the "T" is silent, so it sounds like "sorbay" not pronouncing the "T".

There are several delicious sorbet flavors, e.g., lime, raspberry, mango, cherry, blackberry, etc. My favorite is mango.

Sorbet is like ice cream, however, it is non-dairy. There is no milk at all. Now, sorbet is used to cleanse our palates in our mouth during our dining experience.

OUR PALATES

Ok, let's discuss it. In our mouths are two palates. Notice the spelling. I am not saying palettes like palettes of colors. I am saying palates that are found in the mouth.

We have a hard palate and a soft palate. Here is where you find the palates in your mouth. Place your tongue at the roof of your mouth, where you feel all the hardness. That is your hard palate. Then move your tongue back close to your throat, where you feel the soft fleshy area. That is your soft palate.

When enjoying a multiple-course meal, it is always good to have sorbet to cleanse your palates to prepare you for your main course, the entrée. Here is how it works. If you've had soup, salad, or any appetizer or hors d'oeuvres prior to your entrée, you would order sorbet to cleanse the taste of the soup, salad, etc. from your palates to prepare them for your main course, which is your entrée. Remember, food will not only land on your tongue to allow you to taste it; it goes on your palates as you consume it. So, it is not just about the taste buds on your tongue; it's about the whole anatomy of the mouth that should be considered when enjoying your meal.

Now, you would not order sorbet if you've only ordered an entrée or if you are not eating anything prior to the entrée because the sorbet is to cleanse the palates to prepare your mouth to enjoy the main course. If you had nothing before the entrée, there is nothing to cleanse from your palates.

Keep in mind that you will likely not find restaurants that are 1–4-star rating serve sorbet because it is commonly served in 5 or higher star restaurants. So, don't be disappointed when you visit your nearby everyday restaurant and they do not serve it. Also, keep in mind sorbet is not an automatic course. Yes, it's a course. It would be something you order, and yes, you must pay for it. It is usually a menu item. However, if you are in an upscale restaurant and you don't see it on the menu, feel free to ask if they serve sorbet.

You may not see many folks order or eat sorbet when you visit upscale restaurants. It is not because they don't desire it. In many cases, it's because they are not aware of such a thing. I've been in restaurants, and even the server believes it is dessert. I would pleasantly inform them of the actual purpose of sorbet, and they would be enlightened and thank me for the kind explanation. Don't get me wrong, if you desire sorbet as dessert, have at it. It is your meal, and you are paying for it. Because I don't consume dairy, sometimes, I order sorbet again for dessert after using it to cleanse my palates. So, don't feel weird if you desire to order it again for dessert. I just want to be sure you are aware of the essential purpose of sorbet.

The next time you dine in an upscale restaurant, don't be afraid to order your sorbet. You deserve the experience. Have fun!

SECRET CODES

While dining, especially in an upscale restaurant or formal dining room on a cruise ship, there are secret codes, which allow you to indirectly communicate with the server. You would do that with your napkin and flatware. The positioning of both will determine the server's next step in assisting you.

In most upscale restaurants, the server would not need to guess or ask when you leave the table to use the restroom if you will return or if you're finished because your napkin and utensils will tell them.

When you are in the everyday 1–4-star restaurants, those secret codes may not be effective because the staff may not have been taught to understand or be cognizant of those codes.

There are essentially two different types of codes, the American Style, and the European Style. Let's discuss them.

AMERICAN STYLE SECRET CODES

When dining in American style and you must leave the table for any reason with plans to return to finish your meal, it is important to place your utensils in the pause position.

This position is when your knife lays at the top of your plate with the handle on the right. When you place that knife at the top, be sure the jagged edge faces you. You should never have the jagged edge facing another guest. That is perceived to be offensive.

Your fork should be placed between 4:20 and 5, facing upward. I like to remain consistent, so I recommend placing your fork in the 5 o'clock position. Also, be sure the handle of the fork is slightly hanging off the plate. Don't place it at a tilt. It should not touch the table because it has been used.

When dining, always consider your plate to be a big round clock. Therefore, when determining the 5 o'clock position, just count from 12 to 5, where you would position the fork.

Now, this position communicates to the server that you will return to complete your course; do not take it or clear your area. This is very important. Before knowing this rule years ago, I experienced leaving my table for a run to the restroom, and when I returned, my food was gone. I was so disturbed because the food was delicious, and I really looked forward to completing it. Not to mention, I wanted to get my money's worth and eat the full portion. LOL That was not a good experience. Remember, use the pause position if you will return.

The secret code is pretty simple when you are finished and will definitely communicate a message to the server. Since your knife is already at the top for pausing or resting, all you must do is place your fork in the 5 o'clock position facing upward and move the knife from the top to the right of the fork, with both handles hanging off, side by side. Be sure the jagged edge of the knife faces the fork. That is the finished position, and that communicates to the server you are finished.

The paused and finished positions are the two most used and are understood by most upscale servers.

AMERICAN PAUSED POSITION

AMERICAN FINISHED POSITION

EUROPEAN STYLE SECRET CODES

This style is a bit different because of culture. While dining, the same scenario may take place where you need to use the restroom. To place your utensils in the pause position, you would need to place your knife on the right at the 4:20 position with a jagged edge facing you, and the fork at the 7:40 position, sort of like an upside-down V. The fork should face downward and overlap the top of the knife about ¼ down from the top. This position communicates to the server that you will return, do not remove your items.

Once you are finished, both utensils will be positioned at the 5 o'clock position just like the American style, except the fork faces downward. That position communicates to the server that you are finished.

EUROPEAN PAUSED POSITION

EUROPEAN FINISHED POSITION

NAPKIN SECRET CODES

Napkin secret codes are simple as well. When you have paused and have left your seat with the intention to return, you not only place your utensils in the pause position, you place your napkin on your seat as well. That, too, communicates to the server you will return. Do not remove your items or food.

If the server notices the positioning of the utensils and the napkin, they will more than likely, take the napkin, fold it nicely, and place it on the left of your plate. That's typical.

Now, when you are finished, simply place the napkin on the left of your plate and your utensils in the finished position. No need for fancy folding or design of your napkin. Simply place it on the left of your plate. Once your utensils and napkin are in these positions, it is clear to the server, you are finished, and they may remove everything.

There is no need for them to ask if you are finished. Your items have indicated to them that you are finished.

TABLE SETTINGS

When you sit at a table, typically everything you will need to enjoy the foods served are at your placement. With that said, no hands in your food. You will have a utensil for everything you will eat. Therefore, keep your hands out of your food unless it is finger food. Even then, there is a way to eat without being very messy or having everything all over your hands. Let's discuss a few settings to fully understand them.

INFORMAL OR BASIC SETTING

When setting the table, you set according to the courses you will have, whether it be at home or in a restaurant. Generally, if in a restaurant, you will receive each course one at a time. So, the dishes will be placed in front of you one at a time. Let's work with the scenario that you will have a private three-course dinner party at home, and you would like to set the table indicating the courses your guests will have. They will be served:
- Soup
- Salad
- Entrée

When setting the table for a basic setting, you will have a salad fork and an entrée fork on the left of your plate. Keep in mind that forks are always on the left except if you are having shellfish, you will have a small fork on the right of the knife and spoon. Otherwise, forks are on the left. Keep in mind the salad fork is typically smaller than the entrée fork. However, if you do not have a small and large fork, it's fine the salad and entrée forks are the same size. They are usually placed in position where the salad fork is slightly higher than the entrée fork as they are placed side-by-side. To know which fork is the salad fork at any given time, it is the fork farthest from the plate on the outside in a typical setting. If there are three forks, one for fish, the salad fork more than likely, will be the fork immediately left of the entrée fork. So, never doubt which fork is for the salad. Obviously, the fork nearest to the plate is the entrée fork. You will see this too in a restaurant.

Let's head over to the right of the plate. There, you will place the entrée knife to accompany the entrée fork. You may also provide a second knife right next to the entrée knife to accompany the salad fork. That would be the salad knife. There are times when enjoying salad, that you need to cut the lettuce, cucumbers, etc. That is why the knife is provided. Oh, and remember, the jagged edge of both knives faces the plate.

On the right of the knife will be the soup spoon because we are having soup. Therefore, the soup spoon should be there as well. If you plan to have coffee or tea, the teaspoon will be either between the knife and soup spoon, or some folks will place it on the right of the soup spoon.

At the tip of the knife should be a water goblet. That is a stem glass only for water or juice. It is not for adult beverages, only water or juice.

In the middle, you will place your charger if you decide to add one to accentuate the table. If there is not a charger plate, the first plate will be your entrée plate. On top of the entrée plate will be your salad plate, and because you're having soup, your soup bowl will be on top of the salad plate.

The napkin may be placed anywhere in the center or on the left, not the right. This is the basic setting:

- Salad fork
- Entrée fork
- Entrée knife
- Salad knife (optional)
- Teaspoon
- Soupspoon
- Water goblet
- Charger (optional)
- Entrée plate
- Salad plate
- Soup bowl
- Napkin
- Teacup
- Saucer

Makes for a beautiful and simple presentation.

FORMAL SETTING

The formal setting would have everything the basic setting has. However, just a few items are added to make it formal.

On the right of the goblet, you will place another stem glass for adult beverage, perhaps wine. So, you will have a water goblet and a wine glass.

You will place a bread plate and butter knife on the left top of the plate above the forks. The bread plate, in most cases, will be the same size as a saucer. On the bread plate, you will add a butter knife. Those additional items typically make the setting formal:

- Salad fork
- Entrée fork
- Entrée knife
- Salad knife (optional)

- Teaspoon
- Soupspoon
- Water goblet
- Charger (optional)
- Entrée plate
- Salad plate
- Soup bowl
- Napkin
- Wine glass
- Bread plate
- Butter knife
- Teacup
- Saucer

This is an even more beautiful presentation.

MOST FORMAL SETTING

The most formal has all the items for the basic and formal. It has all the bells and whistles! A few more items are added.

Next to the water goblet and wine glass, folks typically add a champagne glass called a flute. In total, you will have three stem glasses. You may even add another glass for another alternative drink. Some folks have champagne, white wine, and red wine. It is a preference depending on what they plan to eat.

On the upper right of the spoon, you will see a teacup and saucer. Always ensure the teacup handle is on the right.

Finally, directly above the plate, centered, are the dessert spoon and fork. Be sure the spoon is positioned above the fork, and the bowl of the spoon is on the left, ensuring the handle is on the right.

The fork is placed below the spoon with the tines (not fork teeth), facing the right, and the fork's handle is on the left. Both utensils face upward. If you choose, you may just place one utensil there, depending on the dessert you are serving. Be sure they are positioned correctly.

There is a reason for this positioning. When having multiple courses, it is a process of elimination. Once you have finished each course, the plate or bowl, and utensil are collected. As you dine and eliminate your courses, the final course, in many cases, is the dessert, if it will be served. Therefore, only the dessert utensils are left. At which time, you or the host, will gracefully move the spoon to the right, if you will need a spoon for your dessert or if you need a fork, gracefully move the fork to the left. The positioning of the spoon and or fork at the top of your plate allows them to smoothly move the item without flipping them over. That is why the dessert utensils must be positioned the way I've advised. There is a method to everything in etiquette. I just love it.

Let's recap what the typical most formal setting entails:
- Salad fork
- Entrée fork
- Entrée knife
- Salad fork
- Teaspoon
- Soupspoon
- Water goblet
- Wine glass
- Champagne flute
- Charger (optional)
- Entrée plate
- Salad plate
- Soup bowl
- Napkin
- Bread plate
- Butter knife
- Dessert spoon
- Dessert fork
- Teacup
- Saucer

Absolutely beautiful!

MOST FORMAL SETTING

Of course, there are occasions when the setting is much more extravagant. It all depends on the number of courses you will have. There are instances and occasions when the guests will have much more than five courses. Remember, there is a utensil and plate or bowl for every course, depending on what is needed.

WHAT'S YOURS ON THE TABLE

I love to cruise. My family and I have traveled the world via cruise ships. We enjoy dining in the formal dining room. We look forward to the formal nights when we dress up, take photos, and enjoy a delicious multiple-course meal.

However, before entering the fabulous etiquette industry, I was often confused about which glass was mine or which bread plate was mine. I lacked confidence. I often used my neighbor's glass or bread plate and always apologized after realizing it was theirs. Those were certainly faux pas moments.

After educating myself about it and receiving formal education on all things etiquette, I realized the error made. To be honest with you, I was quite ashamed. Nonetheless, I am so very happy to know, without a doubt, which is mine.

So, if you sit at a table and feel a bit confused, not knowing which glass or bread plate is yours, you have a couple of methods to help.

1. You can use this acronym, B.M.W. That stands for Bread, Meal, Water. That means your bread is on the left, meal in the middle, and water(drinks) on the right. Many seem to use this acronym, and it works.

2. Another way you can be sure, is by holding the ok sign on both hands under the table for your view only. When you make the ok sign with the right hand, the thumb and index finger touch at the tips, making a circle. The third, fourth, and pinky fingers are pointed straight up; you will notice you just made a "d". When you do the same with your left hand, it will make a "b". That is telling you, bread on the left and drinks on the right.

Once you begin to use either one of these methods, you will be certain you are using your items and not your neighbor's. I wish I could see you the next time you dine and utilize one of these methods. You may have to use one for a while until you are completely comfortable with this piece of information. Don't ever be ashamed to use them. Trust me; it's more embarrassing when you use your neighbor's item. LOL Not good!

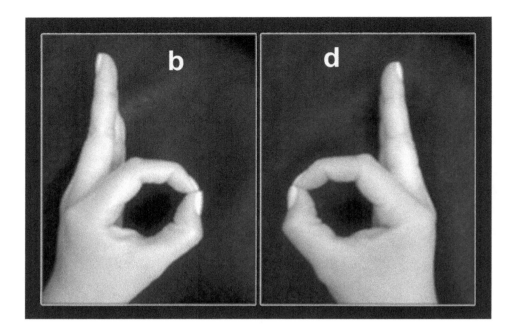

ENJOYING SOUP

Yes, sometimes I will visit a restaurant just for their soup. It could be puree or have chunks of food depending on the culture. My palates are pleased when I have tomato soup. There's something about that taste. When I enjoy my soup, I want to ensure there is no dripping from my spoon.

So, allow me to share how to prevent the dripping. The proper way to enjoy your soup gracefully is to use your spoon and scoop from the middle, then move the spoon away from you while scooping, run it on the ledge of the bowl to be rid of the liquid on the bottom, then bring it to your mouth. By the time you scoop away, run it on the ledge, and bring it to you, the dripping is over, and you can gracefully enjoy the soup without having any of it fall on your clothes or run down your lip or chin.

I have found this method to be the solution to the dripping of my soup. I had no idea it was this simple until entering this fabulous industry of etiquette.

AMERICAN STYLE DINING

I alluded quite a bit to the two different styles of dining in previous sections of Table Etiquette. Indeed, there are two most common styles of dining, and they are American and European. Let's discuss the American style first. Before I share this style's protocols, it is important for you to know this style should only be used in America. Using it in other cultures will be an easy giveaway that you are American, and you are a tourist or visitor in their country. If you wish to blend in, practice the proper style of their culture.

This style can be referred to as the American style. Emily Post refers to it as "zig-zag" eating. This is a very interesting style of dining because it certainly requires a bit of a zig-zag indeed. Allow me to take you step by step. Follow closely, lest you miss a step.

Before you begin to cut, you must ensure your index fingers are in place on the utensils. Remember, at the beginning of this chapter, I mentioned to you that your index fingers control your napkin and utensils? Here we go.

When you pick up your knife, you must be sure the knife's handle stops in the palm of your hand. You don't want the handle sticking out the back of your hand. Be sure to hold it where the handle is in the middle of your palm.

Then you extend your index finger to where it stops at the neck of the knife between the handle and the blade. You should not have your finger extended onto the blade because, more than likely, your finger may end up in the food when cutting it. So, use the neck of the knife as your stopping point. You will then close the other fingers to hold the knife firmly.

You will also hold the fork the same way, making sure the index finger is extended to the neck of the fork, where the handle stops, and the base of the tines begin.

Ok, you are ready to begin cutting. Let's say you have a variety of foods on your plate. One of them happens to be chicken breast. It is time to cut your chicken breast or anything else on your plate, for that matter. Be mindful not to cut any more than one piece at a time of anything on your plate. Do you remember when mommy used to cut your food in multiple pieces as a child? That's not what we want to do. We will cut only one piece at a time. That's the proper thing to do.

Remember our settings. The fork is on the left and the knife on the right. Please do not switch them. When cutting, the proper way to use these two utensils is to have the knife in your right and the fork in your left. Even if you are left-handed, your knife remains in your right hand. Remember, you will use both hands, so keep it in your right. It may feel awkward initially. However, the more you practice, the more it will become natural for you.

Hold down the chicken breast with the fork. The fork remains stationed. You do not move the fork. You are holding the chicken breast to ensure it doesn't move as you cut. Also, try to place your arm in a natural position, not having it up high with your elbow pointing upwards. Hold it down naturally with your elbow closer to your body.

Then, you take the knife and place it with the jagged edge down onto the chicken breast. Be sure your index finger is extended to the neck of the knife to keep it in position. It will allow you to slice the meat. Once you slice it, raise the knife slightly and slice again, if needed. This would be repeated until you have gracefully cut one piece for you to enjoy. You certainly do not want to saw the meat. So, be sure to slice not saw anything on your plate.

After cutting the piece, rest the knife at the top edge of your plate where it is out of the way of your food on the plate. Do not, I repeat, do not lay your knife on the right at a tilt, partially on the plate and partially on the table. That is incorrect. Lay your knife at the top of the plate. Be sure the handle is on the right, and the jagged edge of the blade faces you.

Then, if you are right-handed, switch the fork to the right hand to comfortably enjoy that portion with the fork in upward position. That is where the zig-zag comes in. If you are left-handed, keep the fork in your left hand and comfortably enjoy that portion. Regardless of your dominant hand, be sure to place the idle hand in your lap, not on the table.

In this case, we are going to pretend you are right-handed. So, you have switched the fork to the right, and you are enjoying your portion. When it is time to cut again, you would switch the fork back to the left hand and position your index finger, as I explained above. After which, you retrieve the knife at the top of your plate and position your index finger. Do not begin cutting unless the index fingers are in place. That is so very important, and it looks refined as well.

You would repeat this process until you have finished cutting whichever food you needed to cut or until you have had all you desire at the moment.

If you would like to take a drink, remember to place your utensils in the pause position where the knife remains at the top and the fork facing upward in the 5 o'clock position.

Now, when you are ready to enjoy your remaining portion after pausing, you would not cross your body with your left hand to retrieve your fork, that is resting in the 5 o'clock position. You would retrieve the fork with your right hand, then place it in your left hand. After which, retrieve your knife at the top and proceed with the proper protocols mentioned above while having the index fingers in place.

Once you are finished, you will then place the utensils as mentioned previously, in the finished position communicating to the server, you are finished.

This is American-style dining. Remember, eat with grace and patience, following the protocols, and you surely will have a wonderful experience.

EUROPEAN STYLE

The European style, also known as the Continental style, is quite different from the American style. There is only one similarity, and that is how you cut.

Now, this style is commonly used in the European culture, of course. It is also commonly used in many Caribbean islands such as: Jamaica, Trinidad & Tobago, Bahamas, Haiti, and many more. When visiting Europe or most of the Caribbean islands, it's best to use European or Continental style dining to sort of blend in with the natives.

Also, keep in mind while dining in the European style, you should not hide your hands. Unlike the American style that allows you to place your idle hand in your lap, the European style calls for you never to hide your hands. Therefore, if you are not using your utensils at the moment, both wrists should be placed at the edge of the table making a soft fist. If you're just conversing and not actually eating, you will place your wrists in this position. If you place your hands in your lap or where it cannot be clearly seen, it is offensive to the culture. With that said, please remember, if you're not eating at the moment, rest both wrists at the edge of the table to prevent offense.

As I mentioned earlier, there is one similarity between the two styles, and that's how you hold the knife and fork and slice the food item. You must have the index fingers in place, handles in the palm, and fingers closed to have a firm grip on the knife and fork.

It is time to cut your chicken breast or whatever you are having. Slice as I advised previously. Now, here is the huge difference. After slicing, you would not rest the knife anywhere. Instead, rest your right wrist at the edge of the table on the right while holding the knife. Be sure to lower the knife. You don't want to have the knife pointing up in a threatening position. So, lower your knife at the side. Then pivot the food into your mouth with your left hand. Be sure when pivoting, the front of the tines goes toward your mouth with the tines faced downward. During the process, the objective is not to release the knife or the fork. They remain in hand until you pause.

When it is time to cut again, you would repeat the same cutting process, rest the right wrist at the edge of the table on the right, and pivot with your left hand directly in your mouth.

EATING SOFT FOOD ITEMS

Let's say you are also having something soft like mashed potato. Clearly, you cannot pick mashed potato up with a fork as you would something you cut. If you can, then may I suggest something is missing in the mashed potato. LOL Thought I'd make you laugh. Ok, since mashed potato is typically soft and not solid, you would hold the fork face down on the plate. The fork will be stationed. Lower the handle of the fork. Then, with your right hand, use the knife to scoop the mashed potato onto the back of the fork. This is how you would place something soft onto your fork in the European style.

Once you have placed the mashed potato on the back of the fork, rest the right wrist on the edge of the table with the knife and pivot the mashed potato into your mouth with the fork consistently facing downward. You would repeat this every time you would like a portion of your mashed potato or any other soft item on your plate.

SCOOPING SOMETHING SOFT ONTO BACK OF FORK

HOW TO EAT RICE OR A COMBO OF FOODS

This protocol is quite fun because there are several dynamics that you will enjoy perfecting. No stress. Once you comprehend and practice this process, you will probably favor it.

If you have rice or a combination of foods on your plate, you will need a strategy to get it onto your fork to enjoy it. Let's discuss the techniques.

Keeping the fork in the left hand and knife in the right hand, you would sit the tines of the fork flat on the plate facing upward. Again, hold it in place. After sitting the fork on the plate, you will position the knife on the plate, making sure it is between your body and the fork, and it should be parallel to your body. You would not position the knife above the fork, which is what I have witnessed folks do countless times. The knife should be positioned right below the fork. At this point, with your index finger in place on the knife, you would scoop the rice away from you onto the fork. Then, you rest the right wrist on the edge of the table and pivot the rice into your mouth, keeping the fork facing upward. During your experience eating your portions, this is one of the rare circumstances that calls for you to have your tines faced upward. Here is another thing. Remember, when the fork was faced downward, your index finger was at the top near the neck? Well, when you turn the fork over for the rice, your index finger and thumb will gradually position on the sides of the fork near the neck to prevent you from feeling awkward when holding it. So, your index finger will no longer be at the top. It will be on the side of the fork near the neck, just like your thumb. Ok.

SCOOPING RICE ON TO THE FORK

If you need to take a drink, place your utensils in the pause position as mentioned previously, with the fork faced downward and the jagged edge of the knife facing you in that upside-down V position. When it is time to finish your portions, lift the fork with your left hand and the knife with the right and proceed, having your index fingers in place and handles in the palms.

When finished, place both utensils in the finished position, which is the 5 o'clock position, fork faced downward, and handles hanging off the edge a bit.

So, there you have it, Table Etiquette & Protocol in a nutshell. I certainly hope these protocols will transform your way of doing things at the table and, of course, boost your confidence when dining with others regardless of their status and caliber because you deserve a seat at the table for more reasons than one.

It has always been my recommendation to practice at home, and it will become natural when you're dining out.

This was an exciting chapter to write because I know without a doubt, once you have read it and begin to apply the protocols, life will not be the same. Meetings over lunch or dinner will not be the same. Your dates will not be the same, and those private dinners you host will not be the same. Now go and be great with your extraordinary self.

CHAPTER 12
EFFECTIVE COMMUNICATION

When someone of elegance and grace speaks, they make every effort to speak with clarity having the goal to communicate as effectively as possible. Enunciating and pronouncing words are paramount when attempting to communicate effectively.

I recall countless times in the distant past when I would have lazy tongue syndrome. I would not pronounce my words clearly because I thought that was how my peers did it, and seemingly society accepted it. Only later did I learn that society accepts mediocrity in just about every scenario.

I would hear my friends shorten words, and I would mimic them. As I entered high school, I began to notice that my pronunciation of words affected my confidence. When I spoke with such laziness without effort to truly pronounce my words, I did not feel good enough. I did not feel that I fit in with certain groups, like the scholars in school or certain groups of girls that were more polished.

It was then, I decided to adjust my speech. I made every effort to speak properly. That was when my interest in reading heightened, and I began to learn new words and ways to express myself and, most importantly, structure my sentences for clarity. I began to learn the importance of effective communication. I wasn't very familiar with the term effective communication. I don't even recall a teacher using those two words together. However, without realizing, I began to express great interest in effective communication. I took note of how I said words and the reaction they received from the listeners. Surprisingly, my confidence eventually boosted, and I began to feel more comfortable conversing with others at any level. I realized back then, the door to acceleration in life was effective communication. So, I honed in on it. So much so, I began to ace every test and assignment in my English classes. In fact, I graduated at the top of my English class as a senior. I was on a roll, and I knew it.

I began to take opportunities speaking publicly, primarily in church. I remember when one of my mentors in those times, Maureen Sterling, requested that I become one of the Sabbath School Superintendents for our church (same as Sunday School Leader). I was extremely nervous. Nevertheless, I took the opportunity with her support. I was only 21 years old. I will never forget the first time I stood in front of the congregation to head the morning's program. Several of my participants were nowhere to be found, and I felt stuck while standing in front of everyone. I didn't know what to say. A voice told me to just run and give up. However, I looked to my right and in the front seat was Sis. Rosalyn Murray looking straight at me, gesturing to go ahead and skip that item. I read her lips, saying, "You'll be ok." Then, I looked out to the congregation and realized my mother just entered the sanctuary and sat. At that moment, I regained my voice, and my confidence arose, and I completed that program utilizing the present participants. The congregation did not know what was going on in my head and spirit. Therefore, I pretended all was well and that I just needed to pause for a moment. I could not have done it that day without the encouragement and directives of Sis. Rosalyn Murray and the presence of my mom.

I will forever be thankful to my extraordinary mother for her consistent support, love, and belief in me and the coaching and encouragement from Sis. Maureen Sterling and Sis. Rosalyn Murray. By the way, Sis. Rosalyn Murray is now Aunt Roz. Fyi, I married her extraordinary nephew, Jerome. I digress. LOL

As I improved my communication skills, I also began to do voiceovers for different businesses and even answer machine services for individuals and businesses. I was slowly improving my communication skills in a significant way while demonstrating great confidence. I even became the Communications Director at my church and led a phenomenal team as we advanced the department.

Later in my years, I earned a Bachelor of Science Degree in Communications. Taking that step has helped me to have that 3rd eye in terms of communication. I can identify ill grammar, redundancy, or the too many words syndrome in a sentence that others may feel is normal and acceptable. I began to understand the relationship between mediocrity and society.

Here's something I wish for you to embrace and take to heart. Society doesn't see us as individuals with a potential bright future or individuals who have children to educate and rear to be phenomenal adults. Society doesn't see a person who has goals and aspirations. Society doesn't see the single mother or father who is making every attempt to provide the necessary tools for their children to excel in life. Society simply exists, and honey, it's not a personal thing. I regret to inform you that "Society doesn't care about you!" That is why society accepts mediocrity in every case. Society doesn't expect great things from you. Society, people, the public, just view the typical behavior of people and determine that's who and what you will be. Society doesn't care about your background or your mindset. Society generalizes.

So, when you hear people speak with improper grammar and seemingly it is accepted, that's because society says that's how most of them speak, so it's acceptable. Society is not interested in correcting you. You must be interested in correcting, educating, and adjusting yourself to excel or be considered polished, proper, or refined.

Don't get me wrong, I am far from perfect. Sometimes I catch myself saying something out of context or improper grammar, and I literally feel so bad. Have you ever had a conversation with someone, and in retrospect, you realized you used the wrong term, and you wish, oh my goodness, you wish you could have that conversation again to fix it? Yeah, I've been there. It's a tough pill to swallow, especially when you know better. Stuff happens, I guess.

Let's get into the meat and potato of this topic. You are reading this book because you are interested in conducting yourself in every aspect, in a proper and truly acceptable manner.

I often encourage my students to find graceful and proper words to express their thoughts, feelings, and ideas. Try to use softer words that directly make your statement rather than words that go around what you are saying or makes you sound rough. Often, we use too many words to express ourselves and become lost in what we are saying. Other times, we do not make sense out of the words before we verbalize them. Let's look at a few examples of words that are used incorrectly.

- Incorrect: I go to Boyd Anderson High School.

That is an improper statement. If you think about it, if you go to Boyd Anderson High School, then what? What do you do there? Rather, this is the correct way to make that statement.

- I attend Boyd Anderson High School.
  When you attend a place or event, that simply means you take part. You're present. You're in the school as a student.

Let's continue.

- I go to Mount Olivet SDA Church.
  Same scenario: I attend Mount Olivet SDA Church.
- As a polished individual, male or female, instead of stating, "I'm done," one would sound more polished by saying, "I'm finished." It just has a softer finish and a more polished sound.

As I network and interact with various calibers of folks, I realize that many use the words "a lot" quite often. It seems to be a trend now, and many do not realize how often it is used. Instead of using the words "a lot," so often, try using alternatives such as: "Often…, I often say or do…, I frequently…, many people…, many times…, considerably…, extremely…, substantially…, a substantial amount of…, or any other word that has the same meaning and yes, there are two words. It is not "alot."

Let's go a little further. It is never proper to answer someone by saying "yeah." The more polished and refined way to answer is to say "sure, absolutely, or yes". If you are dining with others and one requests a dish or item located on the other side of the table, you would not respond by saying, yeah, no problem. You would say "sure, certainly, or absolutely" and hand it to them or to the person next to you as it travels from person to person on the right until it reaches the person who requested it.

Yeah, is not a proper term. That is why it was never accepted in the old school homes for a child to answer an adult by saying yeah or nah. They are expected to say yes or no. That showed a level of respect that was required. Believe it or not, even today, while in court, it is considered disrespectful to answer the Judge, yeah or nah. That is forbidden.

If dining at a restaurant or in any scenario and someone asks you, would you like something that you truly don't desire, you would not say, "No, I don't want that." The proper way to say it is "No, thank you." If you desire it, say "Yes, thank you." You would not say, "Yes, I want that." It just doesn't sound polished. Same if you would like something, let's say the greens, handed to you, you would not say, "Give me the greens, please." Even though you said please doesn't mean it was polished. You would simply say, "May I have the greens, please?" The objective is to sound more polite, polished, and gentle in your delivery.

Clearly, you're reading this book because you desire to operate in a more refined manner, right?

When communicating, the goal is to be aware and conscious of the words you use to express yourself. Make every attempt to be concise and use words that make sense to express yourself. In no way, shape or form am I telling you to use a bunch of uncommon words or, as they say, "Big words." I am very selective with the "Big words" I use because the average person does not dialogue with those uncommon words.

It is extremely important, as an effective communicator, to communicate somewhat at the level of the person with whom you communicate. I say somewhat because if they are using ill grammar and slang, you should not mimic that. Use proper grammar. It is important you do not consistently use words that the listener does not understand and words that fly over their head. If you do, your communication with that person will be ineffective, and it is as if you are talking over them and attempting to make them feel inadequate in the conversation. A great communicator meets the person with whom they communicate at their level to ensure it is effective.

No need to always show off how many "Big words" you know. Be conscious of the person or group of people you communicate with to ensure you don't speak over their head. You want to encourage people to communicate and have great conversations. So, exhibit humility and kindness and don't dominate and show off at their expense.

You may have noticed I consistently place quotations around the words "Big words" because I don't believe in referring to "Uncommon words" as "Big words." The person who is learning may feel intimidated because I refer to the words as "Big words." They may feel it is impossible to adopt such words in their vocabulary. Therefore, I refer to them as "uncommon words." Clearly, what's uncommon can eventually become common when used frequently. It's a mind thing.

Another technique is if or when you use an uncommon word with children or a peer who may not understand the word, follow it up with a common and basic word that will assist the individual in understanding the meaning of that word to allow them to have a fluent conversation with you. You may even cleverly follow the word with a brief definition. You do this in a non-insulting way yet clarifying your question or the meaning of the word to advance the conversation.

I cannot forget an experience I had in the early 2000's when I thought I was truly on top of my game in communications. I was the Communications Director of my church at the time. My team and I established a news broadcast called MOSDA News, which was used to make all church announcements. We would record it on Tuesday evenings, edit it, then present the finished product Sabbath morning during service.

It was a one-of-a-kind showcase of church announcements. Everyone began to learn about how we presented the church announcements. Our Pastor at the time, absolutely loved what we were doing and supported it tremendously. He arranged for us to travel to Oakwood University Church in Huntsville, Alabama to network with their media and technology department because there was a conference-wide technology event happening that weekend at the church.

I happened to be the mouthpiece of the whole concept and program for my church. As I sat in the great big room with countless tech guys and ladies, I was approached by a journalist who wanted to interview me. He proceeded to ask me questions, mic in front of me and cameras on. I was excited about the experience until he used a word in a sentence I had never heard. The gentleman asked me, "So, how do you plan to PARLAY this way of doing the news to the conference level?" My body felt like fire, and I felt like sinking in the seat. I said to myself, oh my goodness, I have never heard this word, and I don't want to look like a fool on camera. Everyone is watching. Immediately following that thought, a voice said, remember the structure of the sentence. At that point, I quickly answered by saying, "We have not discussed that as yet." He accepted that, and we moved on.

My heart was about to jump from my chest. However, once the answer was seemingly acceptable to him and it was in the correct context, he moved on. I relaxed and was able to complete the interview with confidence. I said that to remind you to use words that are commonly used yet sound intelligent and simple, especially when interviewing or speaking with a total stranger. If you choose to use an uncommon word, follow with a basic synonym, as not to place the interviewee or person you are communicating with in an awkward or insecure position. That's called effective communication.

As you continue improving your communication, which is certainly proper etiquette, consider the fact that one should never end their sentence with the word "at". This is very common in society, and it's even disheartening to hear from a person who has experienced extensive schooling. Let's take a look at some examples of do's and don'ts:

- If you are attempting to learn where a person may be, how about saying, "Where are you?" You would not say, "Where you at?" That is grossly improper yet so common.
- If you're curious to know where someone has been, you would say, "Where have you been?"
  You would not say, "Where you been at?" That, too, is grossly improper, yet, sadly accepted and common.
- If someone is staring at you and you wish to know why, you would say, "Why are you staring at me?"

You certainly would not say, "What you staring at?" Absolutely not. So, the lesson is never to end your sentence with "at". It is not refined, polished, or proper grammar.

These are just a few of the many common grammatical errors to heighten your awareness in terms of grammar.

GENERALIZING THE WORD "THAT"

Another aspect of communication that society accepts is using the word "that" to address people, places, and times. This is completely incorrect, and I am here to remind us to pay attention to the words we use. We have got to wake up because communication is the key to unlocking doors you never knew existed. Let's dive into it. You will perhaps be astonished once you see exactly what I am referring to. You will want to gently slap yourself. LOL

LET'S GO!

When referring to a thing, one would say "That."
- This is the book that changed my life.

The book is a thing, so you would say "That."

When referring to a person, one would say "Who."
- Jackie is the person who taught me proper etiquette.
- You would not say, "Jackie is the person that taught me proper etiquette."

Jackie is a person, not a thing, so you would say, "Who."

When referring to a place, one would say, "Where."
- Florida is the place where I live or Florida is the place

I live.

- You would not say, "Florida is the place that I live in."

When referring to time, one would say "When."

- Twenty-twenty was the year when the world turned upside down with the pandemic. You can even say twenty-twenty was the year the world turned upside down with the pandemic.
- You would not say, twenty-twenty was the year that the world turned upside down with the pandemic.

Twenty-twenty is a time in history. You would say "When", not "That" or not use "When" at all.

Here is a twist when referring to people. If you refer to one or two people, you continue to use "Who."

However, if you are speaking of more than two people, they now become a group, and a group is a unit, a thing. A group is no longer a person. So, you would not say "Who." You would say "That" because a group is a thing or leave the word out completely.

- It would sound like this: The group of people that I addressed earlier, returned to listen again. You can also say, the group of people I addressed earlier, returned to listen again.

Notice the subject is the group. Therefore, we refer to it as that or not reference it at all. The sentence is still complete.

With that said, reflect on the many times you may have used the term "That" when referring to a person, a place, or time. Again, society accepts it, so most people roll with the punches. I suggest you say, "Not I" and leave that ill grammar alone because you are destined for greatness in your communication techniques and other aspects of your life. You want to be the full package as you grow.

You won't be perfect because no one is. However, you wish to be the best version of yourself.

- When you're stating something is yours (possession), you would not say, "It's mines." No no no. There is no "s" at the end. Simply say, it's mine.
- The money on the table is mine.

Remember the lyrics in Michael Jackson's song, "The girl is mine...?" So, when claiming something, take the "s" off the end. Simply say, "Mine."

Here is the last word, but certainly not least.

- If you use the word "Finna" please do yourself the biggest favor, strike it from your vocabulary. For those who are not familiar with this word, allow me to dare use it in a sentence. I'm finna go to the store. Sounds familiar now? Nooooooooooo!!!!! Strike that word, please, from your vocabulary.

That word only places you in a box, and it is not a good box. When a person uses that word, they are immediately judged in a belittling way. They are then placed in a box, labeled, cannot be used. That box is for that business owner who cannot trust you to communicate with their clients or potential clients. That box is for those not invited to certain events or meetings simply because of the lack of communication skills. That box is for those who are misjudged simply because of the one word they may use. Regardless of the usage of that box, it is for people who will be exposed to limited opportunities simply because of that one word.

One would say, but Steve Harvey uses that word all the time. Hello, you are not Steve Harvey. More than likely, you don't have the millions Steve Harvey has, and I guarantee you will not grind and hustle the way Steve Harvey did as he experienced homelessness, toiled and tarried without, went bankrupt, lost everything more than once, and by God's grace, he made it. That is Steve Harvey's story, and there is so much more. He shares in his phenomenal best seller books, that he went through some extremely difficult times to get where he is now, and we are so very proud of him.

You are not Steve Harvey or any other celebrity you have heard using the word "Finna." In fact, it isn't even a word. Recently, it was placed in the Ebonics dictionary because it is so often used by a group of people and seemingly accepted.

Imagine you're on an interview, and the interviewer, asks you, "What do you feel you will contribute to our company?" Your response is "I'm finna do all that I can…" As soon as you utter the word finna, the interviewer, more than likely, did not hear anything you said following that word. He or she has already determined they will not hire you simply because of the usage of that one word.

I beg you, please remove that word from your vocabulary because it will stunt your potentials and opportunities. Trust me. It will!

You may be super intelligent and capable of successfully completing a task or a job. However, more than likely, using that word will prevent you from receiving the opportunity to prove yourself and may cause people to draw the wrong conclusion about you. You deserve to give yourself the chance to thrive. Please strike "Finna" from your vocabulary.

REDUNDANCY

This area of communication is very significant for me because it is overly used, and for some reason, most do not realize the errors. Again, society accepts mediocrity, and this is one that society accepts wholeheartedly.

Unfortunately, many do not listen keenly to their thoughts before verbalizing them. I for one, am far from perfect. However, when I listen to my thoughts at times, I try my very best to ensure I am not redundant with my words. Essentially, it means saying repeatedly the same thing, either with the same word or a different word. I am going to gently remind you of several. I wish I was a cute little ladybug on your wall, witnessing you be in awe as you are reminded of these terms. Here we go:

- When someone says, "I replied back to your email." They don't realize that replied means getting back to them. It's redundant.

One would simply say, "I replied to your email," or "I replied to your text, etc."

- The same with revert back. Revert is going back, so one would only say revert.

"Let's revert to the topic we initially discussed" not, "Let's revert back..."

This one is often used improperly by individuals of all calibers.

- The reason why. The two words mean the same. Reason is why.

Sometimes, one would take it further.

Ex. "The reason why I didn't call you was because I..."

They don't realize that reason, why, and because mean the same thing.

Instead of saying the above, one would simply say; "The reason I didn't call you is due to my busy schedule," or whatever the reason may be.

I truly hope you share the same concerns I have now that it has been presented to you.

Let's keep going.
- Instead of saying just recently, simply use one of the two.

You would not say, "I just recently got home."

One would say, "I recently arrived home." That's it. Or you can say, "I just arrived home." Just use one word.
- Variety and different mean the same.

You would not say, "I had a variety of different teas at the tea party."

One would say, "I had a variety of teas at the tea party."
- Same and exact are very commonly used, not realizing it is redundant.

People commonly say, "This is the same exact person I spoke with earlier."

Instead, it should be, "This is the same person I spoke with earlier," or "This is the exact person..."
- Gather together. Noooo, it's a setup. We don't gather together, or you don't gather together anything. It's redundant.

Instead of saying, "Let's gather together the folks," simply say, "Let's gather the folks."

I have never heard of anyone gathering apart. So, you see, even though the songwriter wrote, "We gather together…," it doesn't mean it is not redundant. The writer was clearly making emphasis. Respectfully, the writer had a reason to use those words together. That doesn't say it is ok for you and me to use it in our everyday communication. It's redundant!

This is one I often hear, especially in a religious setting,

- "Please stand to your feet." Respectfully, one would not stand on anything else but their feet. One would simply say, "Please stand."

I can go on and on.

- "End Result." It's either the end or the result(s),
- "Join in." It's simply "Join us, join me, join them, etc." Join in is redundant.

Lastly, many say "Each and every one." That is also redundant. It's either each person, each thing or everyone or everything.

I know it is painful when you are reminded of the redundancies you may have used, and you're thinking back on the conversations you have had using these and other redundancies. Don't feel bad. I have done the same. You're like, Ouch! Did I actually say that? LOL Yep, you sure did. However, don't dwell on it. Grow and adjust your vocabulary and shine.

The redundancies I mentioned are just a few of what society has accepted.

I encourage you to listen to some of the great orators of our time and past. E.g., First Lady Michelle Obama, President Barack Obama, young Poet, Amanda Gorman, Oprah Winfrey, Dr. Martin Luther King, Jr., President John F. Kennedy, Nelson Mandela, President Bill Clinton, First Lady, Hillary Clinton, and countless others. Take notes and develop as a learner. Always be in the position of learning. There is absolutely no way to develop and evolve into greatness if you do not position yourself as a student.

As you make every effort to demonstrate proper etiquette in your communications, know that you never get a second chance for a first impression. Yes, it sounds like a cliché. Nonetheless, it couldn't be more truthful.

MEETING SOMEONE

Let's go to another aspect of communication.

When you meet someone, you are immediately judged. The person you meet determines whether they wish to invest time into you, even by way of a simple conversation. Or they may determine, they wish not to prolong the conversation beyond the introduction. Therefore, the way you convey your name and the handshake you give or in other cultures, the bow, etc. will determine success or a total crash and burn.

Since I reside in the United States, I will brief you on interacting with someone using the American way of greeting for the first time. Understand that etiquette, especially in this regard, varies depending on the culture. In America, when safe, handshaking is the most common way to greet someone and is primarily used in the introduction process.

When a lady is meeting a gentleman, she will extend her right hand as he extends his. The gentleman would not extend his hand first. He would oblige the lady and allow her to take the lead in this exercise.

If a lady is meeting another lady, both may simultaneously extend their hand to shake.

GREETING A COUPLE

If a lady is meeting a man and woman, especially if she is not aware of the relationship between the two, she would greet the lady of the couple first to show her respect. She would not extend her hand to the gentleman of the couple first. That shows utter disrespect to the lady of the couple.

Once you extend your hand to the lady (lady to lady) and you both shake and greet each other, she most likely, will introduce you to the gentleman accompanying her, as if to say I am inviting you to meet my significant other, friend, colleague, etc. She will feel in control and not disrespected.

The same process is used when a gentleman meets or greets a couple. He would greet the gentleman of the couple first and proceed as explained above.

This may seem to be too much for the average person. However, when meeting a man and woman, it is of utmost importance to show respect and prevent causing either party to feel awkward or disrespected. I'm sure that's what you would prefer if you were out and about with your hubby or sweetheart. Am I correct? Just saying.

HANDSHAKING PROTOCOLS

As I write this book, we are in the middle of a pandemic, and shaking hands is frowned upon and certainly not encouraged. Instead of shaking hands, be sure to take note of the alternatives I will mention a little further in this chapter. Your safety and the safety of your fellow human being is of utmost importance.

When you extend your right hand, not the left, be sure to have your palm open because you will want to lock your thumb with their thumb to achieve a complete and firm handshake. Many folks are guilty of giving a half handshake. A half handshake is not professional.

Once you have extended your right hand, make a natural step forward with your right leg simultaneously with your right arm. They are both moving forward together to engage the person you're meeting. Side note: If you are wearing a badge, wear it on the right. When you extend your hand and step forward one step with your right leg, your entire right side will go closer to the person. At that point, the name badge naturally draws closer to them, and it is more visible. OK

Now let's revert to our handshaking process.

Once you've extended both arm and leg, hopefully, the other person has done the same. Both your thumbs lock in the web between the thumb and index finger. Once that happens, close your hand, and hold firmly with your thumb pointing downward. Shake two to three times and release, arm and leg must then return to its original position. At that point, you may proceed with your introduction and or conversation, or you may mutually agree to disburse.

ALTERNATIVE TO HANDSHAKING

As mentioned, this book gave birth during a pandemic, and I want to be sure I share with you not only handshaking protocols but the alternatives to handshaking as well, to ensure your safety.

These are a few of the most common methods:

- Elbow bump: This alternative is certainly not to be used in a networking or professional environment with unfamiliar folks. This is not the most professional method of greeting. You certainly don't want to go on a job interview and elbow bump the manager. That certainly would not be a good first impression. You would use this with folks you are most familiar.
- The other alternative is placing your right hand over your heart with your palm open as you verbally greet the individual. This signifies that you are sincerely happy to meet them, and it is coming from the heart. This is most appropriate in a professional environment. It can also be used in any other environment because of what it implies.
- In a more comfortable and social environment, one can do the old school wave, "Hello" or "Hi" when greeting someone. You don't want to do that in a professional environment with strangers, either.
- Then there are two fun ways of greeting a close friend or family member. Girls sometimes touch each other's feet.
- There are those who bump fist to fist. This method is also

inappropriate in a professional environment. However, it is cool in a familiar environment with folks you know well or have interacted with previously.

When you are greeting someone by shaking hands or using an alternative, keep these very important protocols in mind:

- Smile.
- Demonstrate Proper Posture.
- Speak Clearly.
- Pronounce Your Words.
- Project Your Voice.
- Look the person in the eyes.

If you have an extended conversation, do not stare the person in the eyes. That's weird. Look anywhere on the face, e.g., the forehead, nose, eyebrows, cheeks, eyelashes, hairline, then go back to the eyes. Remain in that vicinity. They would never know you are not looking into their eyes.

You certainly don't want to look at the wall, floor, or ceiling because you're not speaking to the wall, floor, or ceiling.

One would say your eyes are the windows to your soul. Well…! If I'm speaking with you and you're not looking into my eyes, I may not be able to trust you.

Unfortunately, some people look straight into your eyes and lie to you. However, I am not speaking of those folks. I am referring to true effective communication and looking people in the eyes when communicating with them or in the vicinity of the eyes.

Now, if it is difficult to look someone in the eyes, the issue can be a bit deeper. It may be that the person you are speaking with intimidates you. Well, I'm here to remind you that you should never allow anyone to intimidate you because "YOU ARE GOOD ENOUGH"! Earlier in this book, I reminded you that the person you are speaking with is no more deserving to be in the room or have a seat at the table than you are. No one is any better than you. Embrace the TRUTH that no one, I mean no one, is any better than you, and look the person in the eyes and effectively communicate with them because YOU ARE GOOD ENOUGH! Show that confidence that will open doors of opportunities for you. Don't allow another person to cause you to shrink and not shine like the extraordinary person you are. Rise to the occasion and speak with confidence, demonstrating the protocols I advised and watch what happens.

THE INTRODUCTIONS

When introducing yourself, be sure to say hello, "I'm, or I am" and proceed with your first and last name. Please do not say, Hello, my name is…" That is incorrect. There goes the redundancy again. My name and saying your name is being redundant. The most professional way to reveal your name is to simply say "I'm…).

E.g., "Hello, I'm Jackie Vernon-Thompson."

I would not say, "Hello, my name is Jackie Vernon-Thompson."

The latter sounds quite elementary compared to the first. Don't be influenced when you hear top executives or fellow professionals say "My name is…" They may not have been exposed to this transformative protocol. When you know better, it's always encouraged to do better. So, from now on, I recommend you introduce yourself by saying "I'm...", not "My name is."

It is extremely important to listen to what the person you are meeting is saying during the introduction process. Two things happen when you listen keenly to what they say: you learn how to address them because they will disclose to you exactly how to address them. Secondly, you will be able to respond to them appropriately.

Here's what I mean, when I shake your hand, I may not reveal my name immediately. I may ask, "How are you?" If you are not listening and assuming the interaction will be like most where the name is initially revealed, you may proceed by sharing your name instead of answering my questions. Wait a minute, I ask. "How are you?" Now you're telling me your name? Clearly, you are not listening or focused on our brief experience.

Instead, when I ask, "How are you?" Your response should be, "I'm doing well" or "I'm great" or something like that. Then you exchange the courtesy by asking the same, "And how are you" or simply, "And you?" They will answer and may say, "Thank you for asking." You would then say, "You're welcome" or "My pleasure." That's called small talk and exchanging courtesy.

Once the small talk is out of the way, the next step is to reveal the names. One can simply say, I'm... and you say I'm... Then, one would say, "It's so nice to meet you." The other would say, "Nice to meet you as well." It's that simple.

COMPLIMENTS

If you continue to converse, you may be given a compliment. It is extremely important you accept the compliment with such gratitude that it makes the person who gave the compliment feel extremely happy they made you happy. Be very aware of how you accept compliments because your acceptance or lack thereof can cause that person to feel very awkward to the point where they don't ever wish to give you another compliment.

Again, you are worthy of the finer things in life because YOU ARE GOOD ENOUGH. Gentleman, lady, take that compliment with grace and gratitude. Someone literally took the time to acknowledge something about you and is gracious and confident enough to verbalize it. As an effective communicator and one who demonstrates etiquette, you must receive the compliment with gratitude.

- An incorrect way to accept a compliment is similar to this dialogue
- Random Person: I love your hair.

You: Oh, really, I think it's such a mess. I can't wait to go home to wash it.

Oh noooo that's horrible. You just made the person, especially if you are not familiar with them, feel really awkward and you send the message that you clearly do not feel worthy of the compliment.

Instead, it should sound like this.

- Random Person: I love your hair.
- You: Oh thank you so much. I really appreciate it.

Both smiling and feeling great.

Now, the ideal is to exchange a compliment. However, it is extremely important you are authentic with your compliments. People can smell a fake compliment a mile away, especially ladies. Ladies, am I correct? We have that radar for fakeness. LOL

THE IDEAL:

- Random Person: I love your hair.
- You: Thank you so much. I love your shoes.

Of course, it can be anything you find you like.

By the way, when you compliment someone on something like their dress or shoes, don't ask where they bought it. That's improper. Now, some may volunteer the information; that's different. However, don't say, where did you buy your dress, etc.? She/he may not desire for you to wear the same shoes, dress, purse, suit, etc.

Now, let's be honest. Sometimes, you may not see anything physically to compliment in return. Because it is important to be authentic, you may indirectly compliment her.

It would sound like this.

- Random Person: I love your hair.
- You: Thank you so much. You're so sweet. I really appreciate you.

Notice, you complimented her character by telling her she is so sweet and you expressed gratitude. You did not have to compliment anything physical, if at the time, you did not truly see something to compliment. Remember, authenticity!

You telling her she is so sweet and kind along with the expression of gratitude with a big smile is perfectly fine and leaves her happy that she placed a smile on your face, and you are happy, you placed a smile on her face. Mission accomplished with grace and kindness.

While discussing this topic in one of my Certification Master Classes, one of my phenomenal students reminded us that saying you're so kind lends to complimenting, and she is absolutely correct. I just love my consultants.

RESPECTING HONORIFICS

It is also incredibly important, when meeting someone, to acknowledge the title one may use when introducing themselves. This is another reason it is crucial to listen carefully. If someone introduces themselves with an honor, or a title, it is respectful to use that title with their name when addressing them, e.g., Doctor, Chief, Pastor, Bishop, Lieutenant, Sergeant, etc.

Effective communicators take the time to listen for any specific honor to ensure they address the individual with the proper honorific. Never disregard the title the person mentioned they've earned and address them as Miss, Ms., or Mr. Your conversation should sound similar to this.
- You: Hello, I'm Tabatha.
- Guest: Hi Tabatha, I'm Dr. Thompson
- You: It's a pleasure to meet you, Dr. Thompson.

It is also important to make every attempt to remember the person's name during the conversation and, of course, following. Here is a strategy to remember a person's name. While conversing with them, get comfortable with mentioning the person's name a few times. One thing's for sure, most people love to hear their name. It not only strokes their ego or makes them feel special, it also helps you to remember their name because you have heard yourself say it a few times. I am not saying you should say the person's name every other word. Wherever you can use it in the right context and not seem overbearing, feel free to use it to help you remember.

Respecting honorifics and addressing a person correctly certainly takes you to the top of the etiquette ladder.

I know you may have the question, "Well, suppose you forget their name and see them a week or two later or years down the line. What do you do then?" Here are a few strategies I suggest:

- When you see them, don't make them feel you do not remember them because everyone would like to know they were important enough to be remembered. If the person approaches you, welcome them with a huge smile and greet them. They may engage in a conversation with you while you are just wracking your brain trying to remember their name. You know the face, but you don't remember the name. If you're lucky, you can have a wonderful conversation, and you both depart saying, "Good to see you," and everything worked out. You were saved.

- When you are approached by the individual, again greet them with a welcoming smile, as always. It is typical to engage in a conversation. Now, here is where it gets tricky. The individual may say, "Take my number, so we can connect later." This happens quite often in networking events and professional occasions. You're saying, "Omgoodness! I don't know her/

his name. What do I do?" At that very moment, there are a couple of things you can do.

- You can hand them your cell phone and ask them to input their information to ensure everything is correct. Then you say, "Make sure you input your first and last name as well, please." Boom, you got it. Look at your phone as soon as they input the information. Then, say, "It was great to see you __their name__," and go about your day. No offense made.
- Or you can ask them for their business card.
- You can even say, "Please spell your first name."
- The worst scenario is when the conversation calls for you to use their name or speak on something personal, and you must ask for their first name. Simply say something along these lines, "Please forgive me, I have interacted with so many phenomenal people, please share with me your first name again."

The latter would be the last option. I am always happy when the first scenario was the reality. Usually, after conversing with the person, I would ask someone I know well to remind me of the person's name, and I feel at ease at that point.

So, I advise, during the initial conversation with the person, try to use their name a few times to help you remember and, most of all, be present in the conversation to ensure you have made them feel you were listening.

ADDRESSING A LADY

Finally, when addressing a lady, keep in mind it is easy to offend her by addressing her incorrectly. Don't become agitated about that statement. Allow me to elaborate. My basic definition of etiquette is conducting yourself in a way that doesn't offend others. With that said, you want to communicate in a way that certainly will not offend a lady. Allow me to simplify it for you.

- When a lady is married, everyone knows, she is addressed as **Mrs**.

Now, here is something that seems to be confusing to some. Therefore, they generalize it.

- If a lady has NEVER been married, you will address her as **Miss**. Notice the keyword is NEVER. If she has never been married, she is Miss.

Let's go a little further.

- If you have no idea of her marital status, you will address her as **Ms**. And be sure that "S" sounds like a "Z", or it may sound like Miss. This is if you don't know whether she is married or not. Ms. is the universal way one would address a woman whether she is married or not.
- **Ms**. is also how you would address a lady in a professional environment because no one needs to know her marital status.
- If a lady is divorced, technically, she is now **Ms**. However, if she prefers to be addressed as Mrs., due to respect, address her as Mrs.
- If a lady becomes a widow, she is now technically Ms. However, it is traditional for the lady to maintain her married name until or if she remarries or changes her name back to her maiden name.

If she chooses to be addressed as Mrs., it is proper to respect her request.

Keep in mind that everyone handles experiences differently. As an effective communicator, we respect the request and address her the way she expresses to you is her preference.

BE OPTIMISTIC AND DON'T COMPLAIN

As we discuss effective communication, we must remember that when experiencing challenges in life, we sometimes become tempted to regurgitate everything that's going on. Some may say it's venting. It is advisable to be selective with whom you vent or share your troubles.

Please refrain from complaining when you are in a professional environment or attending an occasion where the energy is up and clearly there is no room for woes in the conversations. When you meet someone, and they ask, "How are you," simply answer with "I'm doing well" or "I can't complain," even though you can. LOL This is in a professional environment.

Understand that people do not like to communicate with someone who always complains. Listen, we all have issues in our lives. We all face challenges. However, we all don't share them with everyone to bring the spirit of that person down. When meeting someone, you should express energy, positivity, and kindness. Be an optimist, not a pessimist. Remember that first impressions are lasting impressions.

When you are an optimist, despite your challenges, people gravitate toward you more and enjoy feeling that positive energy. When that happens, you begin to establish relationships and maybe, one day can truly express the challenges you're experiencing to one of your newfound friends.

When always complaining and singing the woe is me song, very few people will choose to be in your presence. It certainly is not encouraging to anyone. You know how they say, "Speak it into existence?" Yes, speak positivity until you begin to believe it, and it becomes your reality.

Besides, how will you demonstrate proper etiquette in its fullest form when you're negative and always complaining? Look at the glass half full sometimes, not always half empty. That's what I do, and it works. I invite you to try it.

I am not saying never take the opportunity to share your problems with someone. Not at all, because we all do need to vent sometimes. I am saying don't make it a habit to share your woes with anyone who will listen. There is a time and place for everything. Be selective with the who and the when. That's all I'm saying.

When you are finished having a positive conversation with a person or a group of people, it sometimes feels really awkward just standing there. You have nothing else to say, and you really wish to move on to another person, and you don't know how to do it. Don't feel bad. It has happened to me multiple times in the past. Here is a simple and easy solution.

Simply say to the person, "It was so great seeing you, let's keep in touch, excuse me," or "It was a pleasure speaking with you, take care of yourself." At that point, both will bid the other farewell with a smile without feeling awkward. That is indirectly stating to the person you are finished, and you are saying your good-byes. That's called taking care of the small talk and pleasantly departing from each other with a smile.

I am sure you see how intricate effective communication is. If you are not present when communicating with someone, you may easily offend them or place yourself or the other person in an awkward position, and that is exactly what you wish to avoid.

Effective communication opens doors to opportunities. Expressing yourself clearly and precisely heightens people's interest in you because everyone is fond of a great communicator. As they say, communication is the key to relationships, and those relationships can be at any level.

If you can honestly say you perhaps need to improve your communication skills, you will benefit if you take action today. Begin with something simple, like reading a motivational or inspiring book or even a book on effective communication in addition to this one, of course. That way, you are feeding the mind and soul as well as learning new words and improving your communication skills.

CHAPTER 13
NETWORKING ETIQUETTE

Speaking of conversations and meeting folks; there are certain protocols you may wish to practice when conducting business and networking. Some of these essential protocols can assist you in making a deal or even gaining opportunities because you applied and implemented them.

Sometimes you will attend an event that permits you to hand out your card or make a presentation. You must be ready, and you must be on your toes with the protocols.

HANDING OUT BUSINESS CARDS

One should always be equipped with their business card, especially when attending a business event. When you approach someone, or they approach you, be sure to greet them and introduce yourself before handing them your business card. That shows them you are not only interested in handing them your business card, but you also wish to know who they are and perhaps have a conversation with them.

Incidentally, if you arrive at a restaurant and happens to see someone you have seen prior and did not have the opportunity to introduce yourself, that is not the time to hand them your card.

That is not the time either to extend your hand to give them a handshake. Remember, it is improper etiquette to attempt to shake the hand of someone who is eating. You may have germs on your hand, and if they shake your hand, the germs may be transferred to their hand, then to the utensil or worse, if they are having finger food, the germs are transferred directly to the food, which eventually is consumed. Did you see that ripple effect? Yep, that's what happens. So, refrain from handing them your card and shaking hands. It is quite fine to verbally greet them and keep it moving.

Of course, typically, under any other circumstances, it is appropriate to hand your card to someone. However, I encourage you to be aware of the circumstance and try your very best to be appropriate and discern the right time to engage in that fashion.

ELEVATOR PITCH PREPAREDNESS

When you plan to attend a networking event or any event where other professionals or business owners will attend, it is always good to have your elevator pitch prepared because you may be given the opportunity to speak to the audience just to provide them with an idea of what you do. This often happens at networking events. It has happened to me multiple times. When that happens, you need to be prepared with your elevator pitch.

An elevator pitch is just a 30-60 second tops explanation of the nature of your business. You want to be sure the right components are included to be sure it is effectively delivered, such as:

- Your greeting and introduction, "Hello, I'm..."
  - Your name, position, and your company name
  - The demographic you serve.
- The Pain Point
  - The problem society is having
- The Solution
  - Your product or service is the solution to the problem.
- The Ask
  - Ask them for their business (Allow me to be…)
- The Call to Action
  - Inform them how they can reach you and access your services or products.
- Thank them for their time and or attention

All done within 30-60 seconds.

In addition, be sure to keep these tips in mind:
- Your posture is upright.
  - Your posture speaks volumes and can signify confidence or lack thereof.
- Project your voice
  - The audience should clearly hear every word.
  - Not only do you project, but you also pronounce your words clearly.
- Make sure every move is intentional and there is no fidgeting and distracting moves such as:
  - Scratching
  - Rocking back and forth
  - Walking back and forth at a rapid pace
  - Walking back and forth throughout the entire speech.
- There are times you must stand still and focus on an audience member or members to help bring the message home.

- Make gestures to help persuade the audience that they need your product or services to solve their problem.
  - This doesn't mean to beg them or say please over and over. It just means to use gestures like nodding your head when you make a statement or ask a question to help deliver your message and persuade the audience.

Finally, engage the audience through eye contact or even walk down the aisle and connect with them.

You only have 60 seconds, max. Nonetheless, you would be shocked at how effective you can be in just that short amount of time. Of course, there are other techniques you can use to enhance your elevator pitch. I've shared with you just a few.

My objective of this section is to just encourage you to be prepared, if only with the bare essentials of an elevator pitch. Be ready! Be ready!

ONE-LINER

Now, there will be times, more than likely, when someone at any given professional event or networking event, may ask you one-on-one what you do for a living. It is recommended you have something called a one-liner to quickly fill them in and not bore them with an official elevator pitch that is most fit for an audience.

A one-liner would sound something like this:
I offer_____(what services do you offer)_____,
for____(targeted demographic)_____to allow them to____

(solution to their pain point)_____.

After which, you may hand them your card or continue with the dialogue.

When you are armed with this information, there is no way you will fail when given the opportunity. So, go ahead and shine!

DRESS PROFESSIONALLY

It goes without saying to dress professionally because you are in a professional environment. Remember, as I alluded to in previous chapters, your appearance sets the tone and is a part of your first impression.

Ladies, wear appropriate length dresses and skirts and be sure if you're wearing pants, they are slacks and not tights or a style that certainly is not professional.

Refrain from showing your cleavage. That is not professional, nor is it becoming of one who considers themselves professional. Not to mention, it certainly isn't proper etiquette.

Try to wear closed-toe shoes. I believe a nice pair of peep-toe shoes are acceptable. Please try to leave the strapped shoes in your closet for another more relaxed or special occasion. It is always great to have a few blazers in your closet to dress up those sleeveless dresses you have or to accent your dress or shirt. There is nothing wrong with wearing an inside shirt with accent colors to complement your jacket or even a nice dress. However, I advise you to be conscious of where you're going and what you're wearing. Be appropriate with your attire.

Might I add, gentlemen, it is always good to own a black, navy blue, gray, or even brown suit. It is important, gentlemen, to be conservative in this manner. You can always accentuate your suit with a nice white or very light color shirt, your tie, and or your pocket square.

Gentleman, of course, make sure your dress shoes are not scuffed and match your belt. These are two things people tend to recognize when interacting with a professional man. I know I always notice if the belt and shoes match and if his belt buckle is centered. These are very telling!

CHAPTER 14

TIME TO APPLY

Now that you have the blueprint to free yourself, conduct yourself appropriately, and position yourself where success is inevitable in whichever environment you find yourself or intentionally place yourself, it is time for application.

- Proverbs 4:6-7 in the New International Version states,
    - 6. Do not forsake wisdom, and she will protect you; love her, and she will watch over you.
    - 7. Wisdom is supreme; therefore, get wisdom. Though it cost all you have, get understanding.

Wisdom is something that no one can take from you. Once you've got it, it's yours.

Oxford language states wisdom is "The soundness of an action or decision concerning the application of experience, knowledge, and good judgment."

You now possess the knowledge. You've been enlightened on the essential protocols to be the best version of yourself from the inside out. To finish the equation, you must now begin to apply them and use good judgment.

I've shared lessons with you, primarily the lesson of forgiveness. This lesson was the most profound I've learned thus far in my life because it freed me to focus on being the best version of myself.

It also reminded me that I am far from perfect, and I too, make mistakes and, at times, need forgiveness. Bearing that in mind, I will forever embrace these scriptures,

- Mathew 6:14 NIV "For if you forgive other people when they sin against you, your heavenly Father will also forgive you."
- Colossians 3:13 NIV "Bear with each other and forgive one another if any of you has a grievance against someone. Forgive as the Lord forgave you."

The great Maya Angelou made a profound quote that I ask you to read slowly and seek full understanding,

- "Do the best you can until you know better. Then when you know better, do better."

Well, you know better now. The ball is in your court. I hope that you apply these protocols and fundamentals.

I hope you internalize every word, knowing that you are good enough to apply them and make the necessary adjustments.

AFFIRMATION

As you travel through life, I'm sure you've noticed there are ups and downs. There are challenges that some would say are opportunities. There will be folks who are for you and some who are not for you. There will even be some who pretend to be for you and prove quite the contrary when the rubber meets the road. Nonetheless, I encourage you to press forward, believing you deserve that seat at the table. Press forward knowing that you are a child of the King, and you too can be extraordinary and be that person many admire, and younger generations aspire to be like.

Take the opportunity to change lives simply by your deportment. Take the opportunity to change the trajectory of the lives of our youth simply by how you show them to conduct themselves.

Now that you are armed with this information, apply it not just for you but also for those who come behind you.

You have the power now to lead your generation and future generations down a path that positions them to be the best version of themselves and excel in life.

In order to do this, you must maintain high self-esteem. That means a daily routine may be necessary. Allow me to share my typical morning routine with you.

- I pray to thank God for a new day, among other blessings.
- I read my devotion and study God's Word.
- I exercise/Shower
- Check my calendar
- I give it my all as I work.
- Amid my day, I seek the opportunity to do something special for someone else.

It is extremely important you have some sort of daily routine to position yourself professionally and position your mind where you can be productive and function at your best.

I also take the opportunity to read my affirmations often to remind myself of my goals and who I am. Here are a few that you can alter by omitting or adding:

- I am energized and ready to perform.
- I am open and ready for any opportunity that presents itself.
- I am confident.
- I believe in myself.
- I have the skills to accomplish my goals. My goals are attainable
- I am smart and goal-oriented.
- It's my time.
- Doors are opening for me.
- I am an asset, not a liability.
- I will succeed.
- I will live a legacy.
- I will change lives for the better.
- I AM GOOD ENOUGH!

You can do it!

NOW GO AND SHINE!

ABOUT THE AUTHOR

When interacting with others, on the job or in a social setting, etiquette sets true ladies and gentlemen apart in significant ways. Through her work as a Certified Etiquette Expert/Consultant, author and community leader, Jackie Vernon-Thompson has dedicated her life to preparing others for success. In addition to becoming certified, she has earned a Bachelor of Science Degree in Communications and feels her schooling has certainly assisted in effectively conveying the information of etiquette to her students.

She is the founder of From the Inside-Out School of Etiquette where she develops original instructional content for children and adults promoting essential life skills including effective communication/greeting, moving with grace and purpose, personal hygiene, business etiquette, body positivity, table etiquette & protocol (both American and European), traditional etiquette for men/boys and much more.

An engaging teacher and mentor, Jackie regularly presents virtually and in person for families, schools, churches, community events and businesses. Her warm and knowledgeable approach connects with both children and adults looking to make great impressions in any situation.

In addition, Jackie actively trains and certifies aspiring Etiquette Consultants through her 5-week Certification Master Class. To date, she has certified Etiquette Consultants in the U.S. and internationally throughout Bangladesh, Zambia, Uganda, Jamaica, the U.S. Virgin

Islands, St. Lucia, Bahamas, Canada, Trinidad and more.

A philanthropist at heart, Jackie is passionate about changing lives through etiquette. Her school currently serves as a trusted resource for the Broward and Miami/Dade County public school systems. In 2017, Jackie also founded Youth Empowerment Village, Inc., a 501c3 that offers summer programming for children 10-17 focused on public speaking, professionalism, entrepreneurship, and etiquette. The program is free for students thanks to sponsorships from the City of Lauderhill, Walmart, ROSS, Publix, several municipalities, and various other businesses. Through both of her companies, Jackie recently adopted City of Lauderhill Wally Elfers Park and donates time and resources to maintain this beautiful local park.

Jackie serves as an executive board member for the city of Lauderhill's Chamber of Commerce. She was personally honored by Mayor Ken Thurston, Vice Mayor Denise D. Grant, Former Commissioner, Howard Berger, and City Commissioners for her work with the Lauderhill youth and the community at large. Jackie was also named a Woman of Distinction by the Lauderhill Kiwanis Club and an honoree for Lauderhill Women's History Month. Grateful to God for allowing her to fulfill her true purpose, Jackie continues to welcome new opportunities to teach self-improvement through etiquette.

When she's not working to positively impact others, Jackie enjoys networking, traveling, and spending time with family.

SOCIAL MEDIA HANDLES

FACEBOOK
Fromtheinsideoutsoe

INSTAGRAM
@fromtheinsideoutsoe

YOUTUBE
From the inside-Out School of Etiquette

LINKEDIN
From-the-inside-out-school-of-etiquette

TWITTER
@InsideOutSOE

WEBSITE
www.fromtheinsideoutsoe.com

EMAIL
Info@fromtheinsideoutsoe.com
(954) 870-6414

JACKIE VERNON-THOMPSON

TRANSFORMATIVE ETIQUETTE

A GUIDE TO LOVE AND REFINING SELF

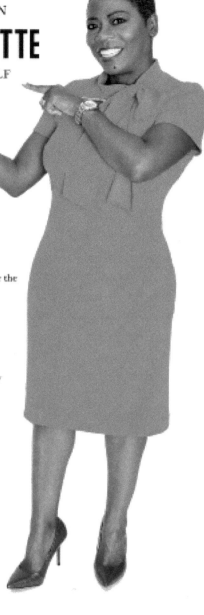

5-WEEK ONLINE CERTIFICATION MASTER CLASS LIVE VIA ZOOM WITH JACKIE

- Become a Certified Etiquette Consultant and help change the trajectory of the lives of our youth and assist adults that need a bit more refining.
- Register at www.fromtheinsideoutsoe.com/certification

ETIQUETTE DVDS TO BE SHIPPED

- We offer eight separate etiquette DVDs on various topics. They are focused on youth refinement.
- WE OFFER THE SERIES as well. You have the option to purchase the eight DVDs in one package at a discounted price.
- Discount Code for 15% Off. DVD/Downloadseries15
- They are found at https://fromtheinsideoutsoe.com/buy-dvd/

ETIQUETTE VIDEO IMMEDIATE DOWNLOADS

- We offer downloads of each DVD and the entire series.
- Discount Code for 15% Off. DVD/Downloadseries15
- They are found at https://fromtheinsideoutsoe.com/download-dvd/

BOOK WORKSHOPS

- We offer virtual and in-person workshops for children and adults Sunday-Friday for social or corporate refinement.
- We are delighted to book your workshop. Please contact us at info@fromtheinsideoutsoe.com or complete our information sheet and select the topics of interest at https://fromtheinsideoutsoe.com/book-workshop/ or call us at 954-870-6414

BOOK AUTHOR APPEARANCE BY EMAILING US

info@fromtheinsideoutsoe.com

FOLLOW MY BLUEPRINT TO ESTABLISHING AND MAINTAINING A BUSINESS AT

- www.buildyourbusinessacademy.com
- You will be escorted step by step, establishing and creating a sound business leaving no stones unturned.
- I will help you navigate the process to ensure everything is in place to launch a viable, trusted, solid, and reliable business. Your clients or customers will believe and know your business is the real deal.

From The
Inside-Out
School of Etiquette
Refining the Whole You

Printed in the USA
CPSIA information can be obtained
at www.ICGtesting.com
LVHW061355271223
767140LV00057B/895